THE FUNDAMEN
PRINCIPLES
OF
YI-KING, TAO

THE CABBALAS OF EGYPT AND THE HEBREWS
(1929)

Contents: The Switchboard of the Universe; The Addition of Names; Definitions of Letters and Numbers; Manner of Arranging Tables for Reading Past, Present and Future Events in Life; Judging the Events; Connection of Names with the Elements and their Action Upon Physical and Mental Life; Connection of Names with Music and the Action of Notes and Chords Upon Your Life.

DIAGRAM OF THE YIN AND YANG

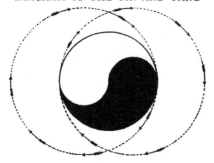

Veolita Parke Boyle

ISBN 0-7661-0082-0

Kessinger Publishing's Rare Reprints
Thousands of Scarce and Hard-to-Find Books!

. . .
. . .
. . .
. . .
. . .
. . .
. . .
. . .
. . .
. . .
. . .
. . .
. . .
. . .
. . .
. . .
. . .
. . .

We kindly invite you to view our extensive catalog list at:
http://www.kessinger.net

THE FUNDAMENTAL PRINCIPLES OF

THE CABBALAS OF EGYPT AND THE HEBREWS

By

VEOLITA PARKE BOYLE

Illustrated by

ELVRITA PARKE BOYLE

PERSONAL NAME RADIO

THE SWITCHBOARD OF THE UNIVERSE

1929

OCCULT PUBLISHING COMPANY

CHICAGO

DEDICATED TO

DR. CHEN HUAN CHANG, PH.D.

The preeminent Chinese scholar of the present day, in grateful recognition of his friendly assistance in my early research of Chinese Mysticism—and to the Great Chinese Nation whose marvelous scientific knowledge reached its peak centuries before the Occidental civilization had emerged from barbarism.

INTRODUCTION

THIS is the day of theories. Almost every few moments we hear of a new cult or creed coming to life and gathering together a small or large array of followers, who rush madly in pursuit of it; while Logic and Reason stand at one side and watch the scramble for the "no thoroughfare."

Those to whom Logic and Reason are companions and not mere outsiders, have grown tired of following "will o' the wisp," and are looking for a *real* road to *some*where.

It is to these wearied seekers for *real* help that The Fundamental Principles of The Yi-King, Tao, is intended to appeal.

Tao—translated—means *"a path; a way; the way of life,"* it is, in other words, the Road to *Some*where in this life. A guide for Now and Here, as well as *the Beyond.*

It will not lead direct to the Garden of Eden, nor make it possible to have all play and no work, which seems to be largely the goal of present day insanity; but it *will* render possible the guiding of one's own life or that of others.

It is in reality "The Way of Life."

To those who have long regarded the Yi-King and the Tao as mere curiosities of literature or as abstract philosophy, the author wishes to say that herein lies the key*; and that it has lain in plain sight throughout the centuries.

---

*The Fundamental Principles of the Yi-King, Tao and the Cabbalas of Egypt and the Hebrews; the Chinese Sacred Science of Name and Number Vibration, through the "Switchboard of the Universe"; including its methods of telling past, present and future, as indicated by it, are fully copyrighted, and protected in United States, England and other countries. All rights reserved and reproduction of its contents, or any part thereof, strictly prohibited.

"The present-day teachings being generally disseminated under the name of Numrology" sayes this author, "are purely elementary in their primary elements to explain or establish any scientific basis for their theories of name and number vibration." The author objects to having the name "Numerology" connected, in any form, with the "scientific teachings and principles of the Yi-King and Tao."

CONTENTS

CHAPTER I

The Switchboard of the Universe

Chart-o-scope of Magnetic Vibratory Action. The science of name and number vibration—The Way of Life—The Book of the Master of the Secret House—The Ritual of the Dead—Vibration-The mystery of science — Radiowaves of the universe—Names, another form of radio-energy—You are a musical instrument - - - - - - - - - -

CHAPTER II

The Addition of Names

The rationale of name-analization —Your name the keynote of your success, failure, happiness or sorrow in life—How you throw your life in or out of tune—The simple mathematics of Name-Radio—How to quickly chart any name—Vowels—Why any entire name cannot be reduced to a single digit - - -

CHAPTER III

Definitions of Letters and Numbers

General characteristics—The Hebrew Cabbala—The Chinese Tao and Yi-King—Plate of Chinese Kous—Numbers 1 to 64—Letters A to Z—The Chinese Circle of Heaven -

~~~~~~~~~~~~~~~~~~~~~~~~~~~~~

THE FUNDAMENTAL PRINCIPLES OF
THE YI-KING, TAO
CABBALAS OF EGYPT & THE HEBREWS

"THE SWITCHBOARD OF THE UNIVERSE"

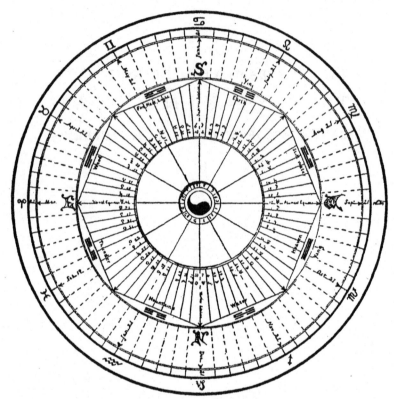

CHART-O-SCOPE OF MAGNETIC VIBRATORY ACTION

of Universal Forces according to the Yi-King of the Chinese and the Cabbalas of Egypt and the Hebrews. Companion Chart, officially recorded in the Library of the Society for Oriental Research (1912) by Veolita (Zeolia) Parke Boyle, and executed by Elvrita (Evarilla) Parke Boyle.

CHAPTER I

The Switchboard of the Universe

THERE is nothing more important or fascinating to each individual than his or her own personal life.

Any one desiring to become a musician must not only have a thorough knowledge of music, but also a thorough knowledge of the instrument he has decided to master.

There are many people who have no desire to master any musical instrument of the ordinary type; but there is not one human being who would not master his own individual life if he could.

You are a musical instrument. Your body, and the conditions of your life, are the result of the harmonies or discords played *by* you or *upon* you from day to day; by your own personal name.

It *is* bringing you good, or it is bringing you harm.

It *is* bringing you strength or it is bringing you physical weakness.

You *can* name your children for success or failure. You *can* name your children for health or illness.

You *can* use name vibration in your business

by knowing the qualities of your prospective employees before engaging them. You *can* judge whether a contemplated partnership will or will not be of advantage to you.

You can do all these things and a hundred more by having a knowledge of the Chinese Sacred Science of Vibration.

The object of this book is to call the attention of seriously intelligent people to a great science involving the fundamental principles of the universe—a knowledge which has until very recently been practically closed to the Western World, for the splendid science of Name Vibration *must* be removed from the realm of occultism to which it has unfortunately been relegated. Its true department is among the vibratory forces of physics; in the same category are wireless telegraphy, phonography, atmospheric waves, and lines of a similar order. This is where it will finally be placed when, like many another science, it has sounded the gamut of skeptical unbelief and the bad handling of unscientific people.

However, we wish to emphasize the fact that name vibration, while of extreme importance to every human being, is in itself only a small corner of the secret wisdom of the ancient Priesthoods; for that wisdom involves, as we have already stated, the fundamental principles of the action of the universe.

It is not a new science as has been claimed by many, nor even a new discovery; one of the best works upon the subject can be traced to 10,000 B. C., but it is *new* to this Western world.

It may be well to mention here, to those under the impression that the science of name vibration, or numbers as it is usually called, is of Pythagorean origin; that Pythagoras spent twenty-two years in the East. He brought with him from that source the knowledge in which, as far as can be learned, he later attained great proficiency. As however, by its use, he and his coterie became very powerful, and were slowly but surely securing to themselves all the positions of influence, they aroused much enmity among those not members of his school. This enmity finally reached such proportions that the school was attacked secretly, set on fire and burned to the ground, carrying with it *all* of the records of Pythagoras' work.

Nothing whatever of this is left to us today except the most fragmentary and sketchy outline, therefore rendering absolutely impossible the construction of *any* Pythagorean method.

This science known always among the ancients everywhere as "The Way of Life" is, however, preserved in splendid entirety in the sacred books of the Chinese, in their philosophy and literature. In a very much more complicated form it is preserved in the Indian Vedas; in the Hebrew cabbalas; and in some papyri which we have been fortunate enough to have *discovered* in Egypt, especially the great hieratic papyrus usually known as the *Ritual of the Dead,* the original of which is in the Library of the Louvre at Paris. The literal translation of its Egyptian title is, however, *not* the Ritual of the Dead, but the *"Book of the Master of the Secret House";* in other words, the great Ritual of Initiation possessed by the High Priest alone.

Numbers and letters call into action certain forces always present in the vibratory waves of the universe, and these forces *do* react upon our bodies and the conditions of our lives, producing the results which we will endeavor to explain throughout this work.

They are, as has been said, *purely physical,* and belong just as surely in the curriculum of the *physics* department of our universities as does wireless telegraphy.

A few years ago we placed the subject of this subtle action of vibration in personal names before the late Professor William H. Hallock of the department of physics, Columbia University. With his characteristic strict scientific analysis, he spent some time in closely cross-questioning as to the investigation we had already made, and the number of tests to which we had submitted our conclusions. His verdict delivered slowly and emphatically is given in extctly his own words: "If you have made as much investigation as this and found it answers to that number of tests, then the force is *there* and has *got* to be reckoned with."

We wish to state again decidely that the subject of name vibration must *not* be considered an *occult* one from any point of view, unless we include under the heading of occult other scientific uses of electrical and atmospheric forces.

It is not a cult, a creed, or a theory; though its treatment by the great majority of modern writers, hitherto, has been entirely from the *theoretical* side.

Numbers and letters are not forces in themselves, but each represents a force which is and has always been producing, and will continue forever to produce, a certain particular action or set of actions, whenever called into play. Just as the force present in wireless telegraphy is "as it was in the beginning, is now, and ever shall be"; though *we* have but recently discovered a small atom of its possibilities. This statement cannot be repeated too often nor brought too frequently to the attention of our readers.

In the correct working of any law of nature there is always beauty but never injustice. If we use it wrongly through lack of understanding, it is our own ignorance which is in fault; and if many of the ancient temples of knowledge have been buried beneath the accumulations of the passing centuries, it is for us to dig them out and utilize their teachings as far as our resources will allow.

Every one knows that sound is the result of

vibration, as we have said; and nearly every one is aware that in the well known experiments of sand upon a sounding board, and in the thousand and one varied experiments of the famous Helmholtz and his brother investigators, it has been proved beyond all question that sound, or in other words, vibration, also produces *form.*

If this law is working so steadily and unchangingly as to produce just as perfect and beautiful form in atoms of such minuteness that we can only see them with the aid of powerful magnifying glasses, then surely is it working just as strongly in the vital every-day interests of human life, and it is for us to learn to handle our instrument so that from our own lives may come the harmonies intended by the Creator, instead of the jangling discords which fill the newspapers of today.

When God created the earth He produced vegetation upon it; otherwise the human life which was to inhabit the goodly planet He had made would have had no means of sustenance.

In like manner have been provided the multitudinous other laws which, as we have gained in the knowledge of their use, have placed more and more ease and luxury within our reach; and this law of vibration, by the use of a few mathematical tables, will work with the same mechanical beauty which characterizes all the laws of creation. Correctly manipulated, it will bring, as it was intended to do, rest and peace into the life of each individual, widening out in this way, by degrees, to the world in general.

Do not understand by this that all labor and effort is to cease; but it *can* end hopeless struggle without result, and deadly sickening strife, which takes the heart from life, and renders possible the question whether it is worth the living.

"In the beginning was the Word and the Word was with God and the Word was God." *St. John, i., I.*

Words *are* with God and words *are* God; for from the *Word* (sound) came all things, letters and words included. Words are the *key* given us to unlock the door of knowledge, happiness, rest and peace, for which we have been searching through time immemorial.

We were not placed upon this earth to suffer in all sorts of horrible ways; and to be told that it will be made up to us in the world to come. It was and is intended that prayer shall be answered, literally now and here, only we must learn to use the *laws* which God has provided for the purpose.

We must repeat: words are sounds; sound is the result of vibration, and as we shape our throats and lips in a certain way to produce the particular word we wish to utter, so does that word when pronounced, produce with equal certainty a form; and as the same form always produces the same word, so does that word always produce the same form.

Names are simply another form of wireless telegraphy. Their message of good or evil is conveyed day and night to the nerves and atoms composing the human body, leaving as well their impress upon the surroundings.

"Sound is movement. Repose is dumb. All sound, all noise, tells of motion; it is the invisible telegraph which nature uses."—*From the French of Rodolphe Radau.*

The laws governing these name vibrations are as accurate as any other electrical or vibratory instrument, producing just as inevitable formations and results as are produced by sun and rain upon the vegetation of the earth.

As the untaught child evokes only discord from a piano, so we, equally untaught children, bring discords into all human affairs by striking ignorantly the keys of *nature's* instrument.

If there is one fact in nature still unknown to us, or forgotten amid the turmoil of life, that fact will continue to work steadily and unchangingly for good or evil, no matter how strenuously we may deny its existence. Therefore it is not for us to deny blindly, but to seek; and if in seeking we find, to carry our researches forward as quickly as possible, thus hastening the time when we may gain control through an intelligent understanding.

If every sound is producing a certain form, it follows as a natural consequence that the *name* of every human being when pronounced also produces a *form.* It has been further

thoroughly proven that certain sounds and
forms being always brought into connection
with a particular person, keeping, therefore,
these special vibrations always about that person, result equally surely in producing a certain
type of being, as well as discordant or harmonious conditions in that person's life.

The minute germs, the sounds we cannot
hear, the myriad things which science has
proved to exist, but which we can neither see
nor feel, show how our lives are being influenced
daily and hourly by millions of invisible objects
from the unseen world about us; therefore, to
claim that we are influenced by a material sound
is not so wonderful a matter after all.

That every building has its own musical keynote is an ordinary and well-known scientific
fact. That every human being has also his or
her own personal keynote is an equally well
known truth among the most eminent physicians
of the present day, many of whom have utilized
this knowledge in their practice and made most
remarkable cures.

CHAPTER II

THE ADDITION OF NAMES

EVERYONE has a surname, and usually a middle name as well as the first one; each of these names has traits of its own which will either modify or increase those of all the others; therefore, while all those individuals with the same name will possess in a general way the type of that name, they will be so varied by the endless combinations as to present an almost kaleidoscopic infinity of change.

Name analysation is simply the plain, practical result of plain, practical reasoning and a close investigation into an as yet almost entirely unexplored region of Physics.

We bestow names today in utter ignorance that there are or can be laws controlling this, as well as every other action of vibration. We produce occasionally, by a happy accident, an harmonious and fairly successful combination; but much more frequently, as always occurs when we are stumbling in the dark, do we bring about disaster; or, at the very least, totally unnecessary troubles and difficulties of every sort, mental and physical.

When we strike a chord upon a musical instrument it must be formed by exact scientific rule, or discord instead of harmony will result. When we form the chord by a name, which is to be always thereafter the keynote of a life, it must be constructed on just as absolute scientific rules; or the life will be thrown out of tune in precisely the same manner as would occur in an ordinary musical instrument under the circumstances.

No science has ever, as yet, been explored to its end. Electricity, upon which so many years of magnificent work has been expended, is even now in its rudimentary stage; and the untraveled regions of the science of names are infinite. Nevertheless, the exact and settled rules already arranged are marvelously accurate and satisfying.

Let us realize that this means removing many of the obstacles, contradictions, and much of the unhappiness from our own immediate lives and those of our children. That it is a guide to one's own good or bad qualities, to those of one's own friends, to those with whom we come into business relations, as well as to someone whom we may be considering as a marriage partner, is a natural law; and last, though unquestionably not least, it is a vital factor in starting children upon a pathway of harmony and happiness, as far as life can bestow it.

THE first step in the science of Name Analysation is to become familiar with the reduction of numbers to their unit. We wish, however, to state that cabbalistic reduction of numbers, as given here, has been in use for thousands of years. It is part of the teachings of the most ancient of ancient Masonry, as every learned Mason knows. It was taught to Moses as an Egyptian priest, carried by him to the Hebrews, has been used by every Hebrew Cabbalist since that time, and is used by them today in many lands.

It was undoubtedly part of the knowledge brought by Pythagoras to his native land from the East, where he was a student for many years; but, as has been said, every trace of his teachings, except the most fragmentary outlines, was lost in the fire which destroyed his school; so there is no possibility of verifying anything in this direction.

In order to give a better understanding of this process before proceeding to the table of letters, we first place the alphabet in its regular numerical order:

1	2	3	4	5	6	7	8	9
A	B	C	D	E	F	G	H	I
10	11	12	13	14	15	16	17	18
J	K	L	M	N	O	P	Q	R
19	20	21	22	23	24	25	26	
S	T	U	V	W	X	Y	Z	

The first nine letters come under single numbers, but beginning with J we have double ones. By means of the reduction used in this study of names, we reduce these to a unit in the following manner:

10 1+0=1	16 1+6=7		22 2+2=4
11 1+1=2	17 1+7=8		23 2+3=5
12 1+2=3	18 1+8=9		24 2+4=6
13 1+3=4	19 1+9=10=1+0=1		25 2+5=7
14 1+4=5	20 2+0=2		26 2+6=8
15 1+5=6	21 2+1=3		

The manner in which we reduce our double numbers is to units and thus obtain their correct positions under the first group, is shown by the table and the final result is now given:

1	2	3	4	5	6	7	8	9
A	B	C	D	E	F	G	H	I
J	K	L	M	N	O	P	Q	R
S	T	U	V	W	X	Y	Z	

This finishes the alphabet, and, besides showing the means by which the table is obtained, gives the method of reducing numbers which is to be used at all times in adding names.

We now begin upon the addition and reduction of names, and for this purpose use some of the most familiar: William and Mary.

By referring to our table, we find that W comes under 5. We place this number under that letter and following out the table with the rest of the letters, see that William stands thus:

W I L L I A M
5+9+3+3+9+1+4=34

We now add these numbers and find that they come, when properly reduced to their unit, to 34, while the unit of Mary is 21, as shown below:

$$M \quad A \quad R \quad Y$$
$$4+1+9+7=21$$

In reading these names, we first turn to the definition given under 21, for Mary, and that given under 34 for William; but we must also remember that 21 will reduce still further to 3 $(21=2+1=3)$; therefore this number will have also the fundamental definition of 3; 34 reduces to 7 $(34=3+4=7)$; therefore this number will have also the fundamental definition of 7.

This, however, will be spoken of again later on.

To read a name properly we must use each name owned by the person for whom the reading is being made.

For instance Mary Alice Williams; the mother's maiden name is Jones, and the *day* of Mary Williams' birth *as a number*.

When, however, a name adds to 11 or 22, it must be left at that number and not reduced to its single digit. For instance, the name Doris and Louis stand respectively as:

$$D \quad O \quad R \quad I \quad S$$
$$4+6+9+9+1=29=2+9=11$$
$$L \quad O \quad U \quad I \quad S$$
$$3+6+3+9+1=22$$

We read Doris as 29, with the *fundamental* characteristics of 11. Louis we read simply as 22.

Having learned to add names in the ordinary manner, we now proceed to a second form of addition to obtain the *"undertone"* of the name.

W   I   L   L   I   A   M
$$5+9+3+3+9+1+4=34$$
$$4+9+6+6+9+8+5=47$$

The *undertone* of the name ($^W_5$ $^I_9$ $^L_3$ $^L_3$ $^I_9$ $^A_1$ $^M_4$) is the set of numbers required to bring the addition of each digit to 9. The undertone of 1 is 8; of 2 is 7; of 3 is 6; of 5 is 4, etc. Therefore the name William reads 34, undertone 47. It will be noted that the undertone of 9 is 9, not zero, which does not function in the number scheme for names.

So the definitions for the name William will be found under the numbers 34 and 47, with the fundamental characteristics of 7 and 11.

The undertone is, as it is called, an *Undertone;* that is to say, an undercurrent.

As the vowels play a large part in the detailed reading of a name, we insert here, through the courtesy of the Frank A. Munsey Company, the following extract from an article entitled "What's in a Name?" by the author of the present work, which appeared in *The Scrap Book*.

"When a child comes into the world we immediately connect a certain sound with it which is to identify that child throughout life—its name. That name at once begins to create about the child a certain type of character and conditions in the child's life."

"There are accurate mathematical rules for the correct arranging of names. Some names from their mere combination of letters are always more or less unfortunate; while there are others which give better conditions. When a name is composed of letters which should not be together, it can often be improved by a slight change."

"If any of the present readers number among their acquaintances those whose names contain a quantity of I's they will find them always over-sensitive, probably "touchy" people, but quickly sympathetic with others. Sometimes they may be aggressive, or, which is the exact reverse, shy and shrinking, depending greatly upon what other letters compose the rest of the name; but the *personal* quality is always strongly marked in them in any case. They are seldom cowards.

"Those with many A's are always quick in judgment and very clear-headed; with too many they will become over-critical. They will be quick in action as well, though this may again be modified by the number of the name. A considerable number of these letters indicate cynicism and a tendency to sarcasm.

"With too great a number of O's a person may be so determined as to become obstinate. He will also be slow about making up his mind, but very immovable when he has once decided upon his course. With an over-amount of these letters he will be slow in movement as well.

"U as a first vowel causes things to slip away; sometimes this may occur because of some fault of the owner of the name containing it, an oversight or neglect to seize an offered opportunity, but frequently it will be through utterly unforeseen and uncontrollable circumstances, bringing much trouble and suffering.

"I's need A's to make them see more clearly, and O's to render them less impulsive. A's need O's to keep them from too hasty conclusions; while O's are always improved by the quickening qualities of the A's.

"Further, everything has an opposing side. A name which gives the trait of great generosity, unless held in check, may produce reckless extravagance; or one bestowing reserve may add deceit, as the instinct is to conceal; while prudence and a tendency to save, though very good and useful qualities, may easily become miserliness. Thus we could proceed indefinitely through endless shades and varieties of character, but the undertaking is too great. It is better to outline the principles of the science, leaving them to be applied to individual cases as they arise."

In order to render as clear as possible the actual manner of using the rules and definitions we give here a few examples of their application.

Taking the name MARGARET we first find

the sum to which it adds

$$M \quad A \quad R \quad G \quad A \quad R \quad E \quad T$$
$$4+1+9+7+1+9+5+2=38$$

Following out the definition of this number, it indicates travel, generosity, too great plainness of speech, a religious spirit and probably a tendency to extravagance.

Suppose there are three people who bear the name Margaret; Margaret Walters, Margaret Johnson, and Margaret Smith. They will each have in a general way the type of traits of Margaret; nevertheless, each will be quite different from the other and lead entirely dissimilar lives. Margaret Smith would be quieter than either of the others; and in some ways might have easier conditions. Margaret Johnson would make the best leader in anything she undertook, have many friends and be very popular. Margaret Walters would be very clearheaded, quick in judgment, and inclined to sarcasm. Each of the others would prefer city to country life, but Margaret Walters would like both, and be divided mentally between these two feelings; because 11 always produces a love for being among many people, while 26, the sum of Walters, having the fundamental traits of 8, gives a love for country life and being alone with Nature.

As each of the three Margarets would probably have a different birthday and possibly a middle name, while the maiden names of the three mothers would also be another item, the characteristics of the three girls would be still more widely diversified.

As another example we take the name Harry. As the sum of this name is 34, which is founda- *34* mentally 7—it tells us that it owner will be re- *7* served; not because he wishes to, but because he cannot help it. He may be an extremely genial person, but whenever anything touches his feelings in any way, he will try to conceal it from all eyes; the deeper the feeling the more likely he is to do so. He will also be very determined and persevering.

Continuing the analyzation we see that he will be clear-headed and very active. The initial "H" H will keep him constantly straining and making an effort. Sometimes because it is necessary, but just as often when it is not. It may be merely for pleasure.

If he is Harry Green, the latter name being 31, he will further have practical sense, caution, *4* and an inclination to save his money. Should he make investments, it will be after careful thought; and the ventures will usually be safe *A* ones; especially as the *a* of *Harry* will add clearness to the mental vision.

If, on the other hand, he should be Harry Louis—Louis being 22—he will spend his money very freely, probably extravagantly. Should the name be Louis Green, he will be wildly extravagant one moment, and subject to fits of economy the next, a peculiar phase of character which his friends will be quite unable to comprehend and which will render him an enigma to himself as well.

It must be thoroughly understood that these readings are the *merest outline,* only introduced as was stated at the beginning, to show in what manner the *rules* are applied.

It has been considered that a somewhat more detailed explanation of another erroneous idea, long propagated in regard to this science of names, is necessary before proceeding to the main subjects treated in the ensuing pages.

NEVER *under any circumstances* add the entire name down to a *single* digit. This method is *absolutely* WRONG, as the most ordinary REAL knowledge of this science will immediately show.

We give as an example the two following names:

James 12=3, Brown 27=9, Smith 24=6
3+9+6=18=1+8=9
Rudolph 40=4, Sidney 31=4,
Darrad 28=10=1=4
4+4+1=9

The single digit in both these cases equals 9, and under the single digit method would give the two owners of these names the characteristics of that number. The real truth is that the two men would be about as different as two natures could possibly be.

James Brown Smith would be gentle, sweet-tempered; inclined to shrink into the background; very musical, self-sacrificing, imaginative, et cetera, while Rudolph Sidney Darrad would be extremely practical; have very little imagination; a violent temper; would be not at all given to stepping into the background; on the contrary would always occupy as large a portion of the foreground as he could conveniently cover. Probably he would have a great love of mechanics, but would be too contrary and self-opinionated ever to rise to genius. A most uncomfortable person to be with, opposing everyone and everything; and altogether an individual to avoid, if possible.

The only correct way to read a name is in its separate parts. James 12, Brown 27, Smith 24, the mother's maiden name—that is the surname—as a fourth item, and the day of birth as a number.

1, 2, 3, 4, 5, 6, 7, 8, 9, are the fundamental or basic numbers of all the others, but each double number has, as well, a special definition of its own.

For instance, the definition of ten will be that given for 10, but it will also have the fundamental characteristics of 1. The fundamental definition of 24 or 42 will be 6, but the most important definition of either of these two numbers will be those given under 24 and 42; 32 or 41 will have their special definitions, but with the fundamental characteristics of 5, etc.

The next point to be explained must be that of the undertones. These will seldom act as strongly in the name as the addition of the name itself.

In "Georgiana," for instance, which adds to 50, the undertone is 49. The undertone is exactly what it is termed; the *undertone*. Nevertheless a name adding to a number which tends to produce trouble—say 23—will be less unfortunate if the undertone is a good one. 23 is either overthrowing or being overthrown. 22 induces giving away one's money; therefore a 23 with a 22 undertone is likely to be overthrown, while a 23 with a 31 undertone is much more probable to overthrow. On the same principle, a fortunate number may be rendered *less* fortunate by a bad undertone.

The initials should be read as an important item, and the most prominent vowels in the entire name will strongly influence the whole; especially if the same vowel occurs more than once.

Taking as an example the name Walter 25, Louis 22, Smith 24, with mother's maiden name Roland, the day of birth the 4th.

The dominant characteristics of Walter 25 will be determination in overcoming obstacles as represented by 7—Walter being 25—especially as the trait will be further enhanced by the equal determination of the 4, counting the day of birth.

The "O" is also determination and this "O" *O*
is in two of the names, Louis and Roland. He
will have also a psychic quality given by the 25, *25*
which number will also make him successful on
or near water. Roland 28=10=1 will make *1*
him inventive, 4 will give a practical mind, a *4*
taste for mechanics and a tendency to work
with his hands. 7, executive ability and a talent *7*
for chemistry; he might therefore, and probably
would do, very original things in either or both
these directions. As 7 gives also a love of *7*
nature, 4 and 22 a passion for travel, especially *4 - 2*
by water, 28 as a 10 or 1 also bestows this *38 -*
quality, he will probably make many journeys
both through desire and necessity. Usually they
will be in regard to mechanical matters, or in-
ventions of his own, or as an engineer or on
engineering matters. 10 or 1 (28) also gives *10 - 1*
talent in engineering, and is the number of the
natural pioneer. The 25 (as 25) will give
strong intuition—if more than one 25 occurs
in a name this may also amount to second sight
—in the present instance it would probably take
the form of dreams or presentiments.

The 22 hates to say no, especially concerning *22 -*
money. The resistance and determination of
the 7 (25) tends, however, to strengthen the *7*
character, and lessen this trait. It would develop into a spasmodic giving and saving.

The 28 produces originality, wit, cleverness; *28*
especially as the R would further this by be- *R*
stowing a strong imagination. Smith would

add musical and artistic tastes; while the i— giving intuition—would strengthen the psychic qualities of the 25.

Louis, 22 with its undertone 32, will give a desire for social life and many friends; while the 35 undertone of Roland gives a desire to be friendly. The natural result of such a combination can be easily seen.

The a of Walter would develop clear-headedness as well as the quickness and intuitiveness; the o's of Louis and Roland caution, the quality of stopping to think before deciding. This combination, therefore, would mean a wellbalanced brain—a man of good judgment neither too quick nor too slow, except at times when the 4 (date of birth) led him into temper and opposition.

TABLE OF CHINESE KOUAS

HEAVEN	EARTH	THUNDER	MOUNTAINS	WOOD	STILL WATER	WATER (OCEANS RAIN)	FIRE

1

2

3

4

5

6

7

8

9

10

11

12

13

14

15

16

17

18

19

20

21

22

23

24

25

26

27

28

29

30

31

32

33

34

35

36

37

38

39

40

41

42

43

44

45

46

47

48

49

50

51

52

53

54

55

56

57

58

59

60

61

62

63

54

CHAPTER III

DEFINITIONS OF LETTERS AND NUMBERS

BEFORE proceeding to the main definitions we present the eight Chinese trigrams, or, in other words, the eight fundamental principles which constitute the action of the universe. The unbroken lines represent the male or positive principle, the broken or divided lines, the female or negative principle.

From these eight trigrams or kouas (pronounced kwa) are formed sixty-four hexagrams, also called kouas, which again constitute the fundamental principles of the forces from 1 to 64.

Heaven the source of all life. *Earth* the mother, producing life and nourishment. *Thunder,* or earthquakes, the starting vibration, indicating the beginning of the vibration of the spring starting the earth to action after the winter sleep. In other words, the vibration necessary to *awaken* life to action for another year.

Mountains which represent the stopping or *sleep* of life; the rest of the night for the new beginning of the morning (or Spring). *Wood,* vegetation, sustenance; also representing *air* in movement, or wind. *Still water* such as quiet mountain lakes or little pools, representing quiet enjoyment, the harvest time of the year, etc. (This is often *incorrectly* translated as *stagnant* water, conveying in our language an entirely wrong meaning.)

Water as rain or the ocean. *Fire* without which life could not exist.

I, OR THE LETTER A.

Creative power, great energy; originality, inventive ability. Happy disposition; agreeable; candid. Usually simple and unaffected. Witty, quick at repartee; sincere; natural leaders. Do everything in an original way, even ordinary work. Regular and exact in detail. Very critical. Strong power of concentration. Inclined to become very deeply absorbed in his own thoughts and occupations, and is usually irritable if interrupted at such moments. Does not like to be still. Generally much travel. Too many A's produce cynicism. It represents strong personality, action and enterprise. Inventors, engineers, pioneers in any line, mental or physical.

Must be careful of the lungs.

Hebrew Cabbala

Will, sagacity; love of science and art. Capable of interpreting and executing the most difficult things. Energy. Dexterity.

In its lowest form, will applied to evil ends, cunning.

Chinese Tao and Yi-King

Reverential; accomplished; i n t e l l i g e n t; thoughtful. Reaches to the four quarters. Reason: He who is without desire will obtain deep insight into the spiritual; but he who is fettered by desire will discover only the shell of things. Ceaseless activity. Active and vigilant all day, treading the proper path over and over. Strength; great and originating power.

Too much force, too much haughtiness, will produce evil.

2, OR THE LETTER B

Quiet, gentle; falls in love readily; spiritual, quick of brain; generally high ideals. Introspective; sometimes dreamers; hate strife, but will fight madly to *protect* others. Brightness and wide comprehension. Do not talk much; often have a slight peculiarity in the use of the lips when speaking, which is usually, rather attractive. Too many B's give delicacy of health because they tend to produce an over-spiritual mind and body. Generally able to measure very accurately with the eye; also good accountants. Successful in quiet occupations, especially where brains and thought are required. Should be careful of over-working the brain. May suffer from headaches.

Hebrew Cabbala

To appease; agreeable and gallant manners. Passion for the other sex. Science; wisdom; knowledge; silence.

In its lowest form; conceit, ignorance, unskillfulness, superficial knowledge.

Chinese Tao and Yi-King

Subordination; humility. Must follow, not lead. Docile and strong to serve man. Manages without doing anything, and instructs without talking. Self culture. In its largeness supports and contains all things. Mild. Comprehension wide, and its brightness great. Sincerity of intention. Regulates and polishes, unites and harmonizes. Indicates adjustment of controversies.

3, OR THE LETTER C

Sees over large spaces mentally; therefore often exaggerates. Talented musically; usually good voices; often very beautiful ones, tenor or soprano. Excellent mimic, therefore good actors. Strong instinct for defending or taking care of helplessness; so make good soldiers, physicians, nurses, etc. Very energetic; often inclined to overdo and thus waste their energies, may tend to dissipation. Fond of children and generally of animals. Obliging; keep promises. Should guard the throat.

Hebrew Cabbala

Action. Give their word; oblige those who are in need of their services. Initiative.

In its lowest form; inaction; frittering away of power; want of concentration; vacillation.

Chinese Tao and Yi-King

Believes in keeping the people unsophisticated but well provided for physically. By this means he keeps them quiet and at rest; gains their approbation and prevents presumption. Strength, action.

4, OR THE LETTER D

Governs the passions, therefore gives a temper. Practical mind; generally considerable common sense, but given to opposing everything, especially anything proposed by someone else than the owner. Therefore usually stands very much in his own light. Inclined to be dictatorial and determined to force others to his own way unless in very exceptional cases. Because of this tendency to oppose and the fact that the temper is rarely well controlled, he is often led into many foolish actions in spite of his general good sense. By this temper he may, and frequently does, injure his own health and life, as well as the health and lives of those around him.

Likes to invest money, but also likes to save, therefore generally cautious in this direction, unless carried away by a desire to oppose outside advice.

Will be most fortunate, and have more friends in the Southwest part of the country, or the Southwest corner in a city. If a man, will probably marry young, but may render the wife and home unhappy through temper, opposition and jealously, may also ruin business matters in the same manner.

If a woman, may spoil opportunities for marriage in the same manner.

A "4" desires to teach, and is very often found in this capacity. They also work well with their hands and are good mechanics. Hard workers, but do not like to work. Excitement will upset the circulation of the blood.

Hebrew Cabbala

Industrious; love to travel by water. Development. The multitudes from which all other ranks are constantly being recruited. Transition; power; thrift; in its lowest form; opposition; hatred; egotism; cruelty; evil.

In its highest form: development of self and others.

Chinese Tao and Yi-King

Advantageous to punish, conduct not agreeable. Should blunt the sharp points and unravel the complications. Should bring ourselves into agreement with others.

He will dim his own radiance and be one with the dust. If he takes the initiative he goes astray, misses his proper course, if he follows, he is docile and gets his regular course. In the Southwest he will get friends, be walking with those of his own class; in the Northeast he will lose them. When such a man puts forth his faculties of destruction, the breath and blood are overthrown. The viscera are injured from top to toe; everything is thrown into disorder.

5, OR THE LETTER E

As the 4 tends to oppose rule, the 5 on the contrary recognizes its absolute necessity and guides the life accordingly.

Its characteristics are versatility of mind,

foresight and ability to learn easily anything upon which the interest is centered. Especially good, however, in anything pertaining to words, writing, foreign languages, etc. Bright, quick, impulsive, nervously energetic, hopeful, charitable. Logical; make good lawyers. Believes in strict justice.

Too many 5's or E's may produce a capricious and changeful disposition living almost entirely by impulse. Can succeed in commerce, science or art.

Apt to have trouble with the liver.

Hebrew Cabbala

Dominates science, occult, philosophy, art, literature. Learns easily. Love for honest pleasures. Beneficence, kindness.

Lowest form: over-kindness; weakness; foolish generosity. Bad qualities of body and spirit.

Chinese Tao and Yi-King

Difficulty in advancing; waiting for the right moment to move in order to gain success. Much speech leads to swift exhaustion. How soon exhausted is a gossip's fulsome talk. Only firmness is necessary for success.

6, OR THE LETTER F

Quiet and calmness are the keynotes of this number. Do not like loud or sudden noises. Excitement or physical strain is bad for this number or letter, as it reacts upon the heart. Seldom worries seriously, but will put aside the

matter until such time as he or she can think
it over in quiet, and decide things calmly.
Musical and artistic talent; good voice and
usually good ear. If the 6 dominates the full
name, the voice will be in the middle register,
baritone or contralto. Love harmony in everything, but often obliged to live in the midst of
strife and noisy or inharmonious surroundings,
which condition wears upon the person seriously
and often causes owners of this number to seek
peace elsewhere. Very fond of birds. Successful usually in mining operations.

Must guard the heart and hearing.

Hebrew Cabbala

Wise disposition. Love of science and art.
Ambitious; successful in love; can gain renown
and fortune. Lowest form; will try to obtain
a fortune by illicit means; covetous; make un-
wise plans which fail when put to the test.

Chinese Tao and Yi-King

Self, in a state of peril, matched against from
without. Contention; strife; wariness; concealment. The completion of material forms. Tends
to produce artists or sculptors.

7, OR THE LETTER G

Determination in overcoming obstacles.
Patience. Love of nature. The instinct to conceal all emotions which touch the feelings deeply
is very strong, making this a number of reserve.
Outwardly the persons possessing this number
are generally very genial and agreeable, be-

coming particularly talkative and perhaps merry, when especially desirous of concealing the fact that they have been very strongly moved by something. Executive ability. Best suited in a line of business having to do with crowds of people; railroads; theatres; politics, etc.

The seat of physical ailments in this number or letter usually lies in the spleen.

Hebrew Cabbala

Patience. In touch with nature. Love of instruction. Able to execute the most difficult works.

Lowest form; deceit, overthrow.

Chinese Tao and Yi-King

One who is free from mind or purpose of his own and does not live for himself. Will continue long, physically and mentally. If he places himself in the background he will be brought forward. Entire trust will be placed in him and his enterprises will be successful. Nourishes and educates the people. Should guard particularly what he sees, hears and says. Can develop mental powers of almost superhuman excellence.

Danger of diseases which are the result of abuse.

8, OR THE LETTER H

This is a number of constant strain and effort. It gives a love for agriculture; outdoor sports and country life. Sometimes the strenuousness is necessary, but often it is merely for pleasure. Taking long walks, mountain climbing, etc.

These people usually keep themselves thin by constant action.

8 produces an easy flow of speech, sometimes talks too much; authors; interesting letter writers; readiness in any line connected with words. Successful in literary work; agriculture; sporting lines; florists, traveling, active professions or trades, or where large crowds gather.

Must guard against stomach troubles and tumors.

Hebrew Cabbala

Agricultural production. Loves t r a v e l, country, hunting. Has balance, justice. Breaking of ties. Represents union of men. Lowest form; strife, ruptures; abuse of justice; dissolution; lawsuits.

Chinese Tao and Yi-King

Contented nature. Union and how it is to be secured. Union to be secured only through the sovereignty of one. Sincerity, benevolence. When possible, very particular in choosing the place for a residence. Mind loves abysmal silence. Chooses virtuous associations. Believes in the government which secures the best order; can get into the most inaccessible places without striving. Quarrels not; so is rarely quarreled with. Especially fond of quiet lakes among the mountains, where multitudes of men do not come. Heart lies in constant action. Loyalty. Danger of treacherous ministers arising, and of excrescences (abnormal growths of various kind,s) growing out at the side.

9, OR THE LETTER I

Produces a deep insight into, or understanding, of life in all its phases; also rather quiet people with strong imaginations; they are prudent, serious, inclined to see the pathetic side of things, but quite as ready to understand and appreciate the ridiculous side. The owners of this number forgive easily, but cannot forget, and can be quickly saddened by mental wounds. They are sometimes inclined to brood over troubles and occasionally develop a tendency to melancholia. They are apt to exaggerate the importance of favors done for them by others, and underestimate those they do themselves; in consequence they are often imposed upon. They make fine authors, and their productions will often range all the way from the deepest sadness to the height of merriment and fantasy because of their strong imaginative qualities. Love music. This force contains within itself the fundamental principles of sound. The middle name of Thomas *Alva* Edison, inventor of the phonograph, adds to this sum. They are especially fond of sad or dreamy compositions, and usually have very lovely, rather deep voices.

A deep love of home and home like accompanies the 9, but the home is frequently broken up or rendered unpleasant in some manner; they therefore suffer greatly in this respect. The 9 is the exact opposite of the 4 in its traits, and while the 4 requires great restraint, the 9 requires, rather, to be pushed forward.

If, however, there are several I's in a name, they usually produce great over-sensitiveness. **If these letters are in a 9 name they will render the owner shy and retiring; if in a 4 name,** aggressive and domineering and exceedingly "touchy."

In either case it will give intuition and sympathetic qualities.

Tendency to separation and divorce.

Physical troubles may come through the stomach and genital organs.

Hebrew Cabbala

Prudence, caution; deliberation. Sincere in promises; pardons easily. Strength and flexibility.

Lowest form: hypocrisy; fraud; guile; over-timorousness; fear.

Chinese Tao and Yi-King

Potters moulding from raw materials. Intelligence. Placidity. Those who grasp too much are likely to be foiled. Scheme too sharply and one cannot wear long. Vanity will bring its own doom. Draws others to unite with him. Rich in resources. The wife is in a position of peril. Husband and wife look on each other with averted eyes. Docile flexibility. Will feel wounds, but will give sympathy and help.

10, OR THE LETTER J

The attributes of a good leader. Originality

in thought and action. Very energetic, constant motion. Good inventors and geometricians. Fine engineers. Natural pioneers. Strong powers of concentration. Generally good health. Clearness of mental vision. Will and force, hope and expectancy. Good executive ability. Generally good natured, happy disposition. Witty; clever at repartee. Must have everything connected with one's work in an exact place.

Too great power of concentration may lead to forgetting others and centering too strongly on one's own personal affairs.

Must guard the lungs and breathing apparatus.

Hebrew Cabbala

Command, strength; curing of maladies; intelligence; industry. Good fortune and elevation from a humbler position; lowest form: ill fortune and fall from a high position.

Chinese Tao and Yi-King

Strength; brilliant action. Pleasure and satisfaction. Propriety. Observance of all rules of courtesy; activity. A path cut straight and level along difficult ground. Humility and wisdom. Undivided attention to the vital breath will bring it to the utmost pliancy. By concentrating his vitality and inducing tenderness, can become like a little child. With proper apprehension and caution there will be good fortune. Faithfulness.

I I, OR THE LETTER K

Very generous; can seldom hold on to money,

so is usually extravagant. Given to telling home truths too plainly or, in other words, making rather blunt speeches, thus often offending. Often considerable talent. Generally fond of learning. Force, strength of character, sometimes rashness and recklessness. In its highest side gives love of study and books. In its lowest, tends to dissipation, and in this case will run down hill rapidly. Often produces much travel. Generally successful in any business reaching into many countries, or to many people. Universality. Very nervous, may at times amount to hysteria. Prefers city to country life.

Danger from nervous strain, though usually great vitality.

Hebrew Cabbala

Strength; fortitude; power; force. Students. Celebrated for personal talent. Renown.

Lowest form: Dissipation; extravagance; arrogance; abuse of power.

Chinese Tao and Yi-King

Lenient towards faults; indulgent; forbearing. Letting be, and exercising forbearance. Fashions after the courses of heaven and earth in order to benefit people. Great, active, vigorous, and at times making itself small, inactive, submissive. Producing advancement. That which is in a state of freedom and repose. Free course.

12, OR THE LETTER L

Sweetness of manner; discretion; spirituality. Intuitive. Sometimes has prophetic dreams, or presentiments. Indicates expansive movement, therefore generally travel. Usually called upon for considerable self-sacrifice, which is given uncomplainingly, but which, of course, means pain for the giver. Loves mystery. Strong tendency to be dreamy. Fond of children and generally of animals. Good mimic, therefore good actor. Fond of music, often talented in this direction. Usually good voice, soprano or tenor, though voice is sometimes weak. Generally requires to eat rather frequently.

Must watch the throat.

Hebrew Cabbala

Dominates dreams and mystery. Sweet manners; spiritual. Bound.

Lowest form: selfishness, the passions let loose. Passion for opposite sex.

Chinese Tao and Yi-King

Repression of the desires. Patience and obedience will bring success. Seeking after strange objects or too much, will create mad desire and change the nature to evil. Therefore the sage seeks to satisfy the cravings of the stomach and not the insatiable craving of the eyes. He puts from him the latter and prefers to seek the former. Shut up and restricted; things are not having their free course.

13, OR THE LETTER M

Faithfulness; conjugal fidelity. Good address. Learns rapidly. Represents constant changes of every sort, therefore brings its owner many experiences. Good in all mechanical lines. Very sociable and usually affectionate nature. It has not, as a general thing, the very unfortunate qualities usually attributed to it by superstitious people. Love of travel, especially by water.

Excitement will upset the circulation of the blood.

Hebrew Cabbala

Friendship; conjugal fidelity; learns with ease. Good address. Transformation, change.

Lowest form: Brings about its own undoing; detruction; new beginnings.

Chinese Tao and Yi-King

Union of men. Elegance, intelligence, strength. To him who cultivates union with men, things must come to belong. Trembling; always fearing. Regard low positions as disgrace, and fear, when in high ones, that they may be lost. Loathing shame. Distinguishes things according to kinds and classes. The union must be based on public considerations without one trace of selfishness. If all the advantages be concentrated into a single source, you will have ten times as much under your command. Husband and wife.

14, OR THE LETTER N

This number represents the body itself; produces nervousnes, impulse, and sometimes poor health, though its strongest tendency is toward size and health. Gives a love of justice, truth, jurisprudence. Talent for law. Clever speakers or writers. Good teachers. Versatile but also practical. Bright and energetic. Generally successful in anything having to do with a mutitude of people. Inclined to marry young, but have a critical analytical quality which sometimets prevents marriage until later life. Sometimes has a tendency to selfishness and an inclination to express opinions on subjects of which they know very little. Learns with facility.

Should watch nerves and liver.

Hebrew Cabbala

Justice, truth, liberty. Love jurisprudence and can become distinguished at the bar. Temperance; combination.

Lowest form: Ill-advised combinations; disunion; giving false testimony.

Chinese Tao and Yi-King

Wisdom, discrimination, strength, vigor, elegance, brightness. By holding fast to the reason of the Ancients the present is mastered. Marriage. The working faculty resides in the eye. Should he allow himself to become vain of his learning or possessions, he will meet disaster.

15, OR THE LETTER O

Usually very modest opinion of themselves. Interested in spiritual matters. Quiet, though quick and brilliant mind; pureness of thought. Versatile; ready speaker; learns easily. Does not like loud, sudden, or discordant noises. Talented in musical lines; good voice, usually baritone or contralto. Apt to take life quietly. Caution, deliberation. If there are a considerable number of O's in the name it will mean overdone caution; extreme slowness in making up the mind, and great determination, sometimes amounting to obstinacy. Especially successful in religious lines.

Must watch the heart and liver.

Hebrew Cabbala

Religious; purity of manners. Love of science and art. Troubles in the marriage state, or in regard to marriage. Strain or excitement will tell upon the liver.

Lowest form: Too subtle, crafty.

Chinese Tao and Yi-King

Humility; subtle, spiritual, profound, cautious, reluctant. Who by quieting can render muddy waters clear. Shrinking; still. Giving honor to others. Regulations of ceremonies. Ingrained ideas. Benign. Friendship.

16, OR THE LETTER P

Brave; frank; loyal; honorable. Love of wresting treasures from the earth. Especially good in mining operations or anything of that type; geology; chemistry.

Determined and naturally quiet. Fond of music, artistic talent. Good voice, generally baritone or contralto, often sculptors, or painters.

High places are dangerous to those having this number. Must be careful of acquiring overconfidence in themselves, as the tendency is to speculate, which in this number will be almost certain to lead to bankruptcy and ruin. The brain in such a case usually gives way.

Hebrew Cabbala

Frank; agreeable; loyal; brave; very susceptible upon all points of honor. Danger of ruin; overthrow; bankruptcy; accidents; falls, loss of position. The mind blasted by the Astral fluid.

Chinese Tao and Yi-King

Returning to the root. Compose music. Should be satisfied with enough. Rises to great height. Gets chronic complaint; lives on. Darkened mind. Should be in a state of stillness and guard this state with unwearying vigor. Live by regular rule. Not to know regular rule leads to wild movements and evil issues. Knowing regular rule and stillness one will endure long and be exempt from decay to end of life. Require much rest. Docile obedience.

17, OR THE LETTER Q

Dominates speech and writing; hope, cheerfulness; love for science, especially good in chemistry and literature. Usually take long journeys, especially across the sea. Excellent number for business, but sometimes do harm by being over-hopeful. Good in connection with theaters, public speaking or also as couriers. Reserved; determined in overcoming obstacles. Love of outdoor life. Very fond of travel. Psychic. Good number for aviators.

Digestive troubles.

Hebrew Cabbala

Hope; insight. Against the torments of the spirit. Revelations in dreams. Love music, poetry, literature and philosophy.

Lowest form: Atheists; uncertainty.

Chinese Tao and Yi-King

Crossing the sea. Going beyond the gates to find associates and so achieving success. Cleaves to the little boy and lets go the man of age and experience; later cleaves to the man and lets go the boy. One who is followed by others. Means the performance of service. Strong comes and places itself under the weak. Attributes movement and pleasure. Simplicity in habits. Distant journeys.

18, OR THE LETTER R

Natural healer and counsellor. Has talent for either a lawyer or a physician.

Great love of home but often unfortunate in this direction. Tendency to the pathetic and sometimes melancholia. Represents the condition of mind usually aroused by twilight in a lonely spot on earth. Strong imaginations, often given to writing verses, usually pathetic; can write very fanciful tales which in spite of the leaning to sadness may often sparkle with humor, as those natures derive great pleasure from the merest trifles. Usually win when drawn into lawsuits.

Genital organs the weakest in this number; also subject to over-excitement of the heart.

Hebrew Cabbala

Justice; truth; integrity; faith; innocence; loyalty. Crosses in love. The twilight.

Lowest form: Unprofitable associations with women. False sense of security.

Chinese Tao and Yi-King

Enjoy even small things. Faithful ministers in the midst of anarchy. Wisdom; shrewdness; benevolence; justice; prudence; circumspection; tact. Should weigh matters well. Can be hypocritical when necessary. May become great.

19, OR THE LETTER S

Thoughtful; compliant, easy to please; very affectionate; amiable; modest; courage in adversity. Love of home and always striving for one, or endeavoring to render it better. Serious, though witty and quick at repartee. Original in thought and action. Often marries young. Successful in real estate or in any matters connected with land, building, etc., providing the site be near water, and especially with low-lying land. The name "Astor" will be found to add to this number. Inventive. Literary.

Danger to the lungs or from troubles affecting the breath.

Hebrew Cabbala

Memory; intelligence; amiable; modest. Supports adversity with resignation. Marriage. The joys of the hearth.

Lowest form: Debauchery; trouble in the home; failure; despair.

Chinese Tao and Yi-King

The fuller understanding of life. Not much danger from water, fire nor high places. Being pleased and compliant. Waters of marsh with earth above enriches and supports people without limit. If he is great he will draw contemplation; he who attracts contemplation will then bring about union of others with himself.

20, OR THE LETTER T

Quick brain; interested in spiritual matters. Artistic; fine draughtsmen. Natural peace makers, but often rendered unhappy by contention in the home. Tends to delicate spiritual bodies, and headaches. Gentle. Talks very little. Thoughtful. Conscience. Given to thinking themselves in the wrong. Often a slight peculiarity in the use of the lips when speaking. Nearly always a pretty mouth. Excellent physicians.

Tendency to brain fever, headaches, and sometimes brain troubles. Danger of accidental poisoning.

Hebrew Cabbala

Religious; chaste; for converting the people. Conscience. Moral. Gentle. Excellent mothers.

Lowest form: Irreligious; weak characters; dissipation; cruelty; drug fiends.

Chinese Tao and Yi-King

Contemplation outward and inward; different from ordinary men. Contemplates his own character. Conscience. Seeming listless and still. Worship; sincerity; dignity. Peace securing. Now high, now low, but in harmony with all.

21, OR THE LETTER U

Sees over large spaces mentally. Quick brain. Natural protectors of all helplessness; good actors and musicians; usually fine voices, soprano or tenor. Very fond of studying the medicinal qualities of plants. Love of gardens; perfumes and their manufacture. Fond of astronomy, literature, poetry, and study in general. Brilliancy. Retain their youth for a long period. Tendency to carping criticism; biting speeches; often very fine singers. The name of the singer Patti is 21.

The U as a letter has a special quality all its own, of having things slip away from it. Sometimes this will be through a personal fault of overlooking or neglecting some opportunity which presented itself. More often, however, it will occur through absolutely uncontrollable circumstances. Must, therefore, when this vowel is the first in a name, or is present in quantity, look over a matter carefully to see that nothing has been neglected.

Must guard the throat.

Hebrew Cabbala

Love poetry, literature, astronomy, geography, and all abstract sciences. Passion for study. Careful in details.

Lowest form: Ignorance; errors; prejudices.

Chinese Tao and Yi-King

The true draughtsman. Bright intelligence. Advantages in restraint. Uniting; but things should not be united in a reckless or irregular way. The essences of things are all within it. Moves by contraries and leads to results opposite to those existing.

22, OR THE LETTER V

This is the number of the "wanderlust." Extremely fond of travel, especially by water. A fortunate number though usually very generous with money, too much so; spends freely and often extravagantly. Strongly artistic; clever; love of ornament; very nervous. Fond of social life; danger of becoming *merely* an ornament. Apt to develop weakness of character because of the money-spending tendency and a strong dislike to saying no and is easily led astray.

In its best side, gives very beautiful characteristics; generosity; gentleness; philanthropist; a natural healer; usually fortunate in regard to money. In its lowest form will become dissipated, weak, extravagant, and drop to the lowest depths.

Safety in travel. Especially succesful in commerce; ships; shipping; importing and exporting.

Be careful of nerves and brain.

Hebrew Cabbala

Fortune; renown; diplomacy; commerce. Influence for voyages and discoveries; liberal and philanthropic ideas. Good counsellors. Diplomats.

Lowest form: Extravagance; dissipation.
Chinese Tao and Yi-King
Occasion for joy. Attains his end. Partial,
becomes complete. The crooked straight. The
empty, full. The worn out, new. Elegance and
intelligence. Society observances. Ornament.
Little advance if ornament takes the lead.

23, OR THE LETTER W

Fond of perfumes and plants for perfumes,
or those having curative properties. Love of
gardens and country life. Versatile mind, clever
in speech and writing or in acquiring languages.
Learns anything easily. Believes strongly in law
and order. Oppression and difficulty; represents
tearing down, particularly tearing down the
house. It therefore brings many unfortunate
occurrences. Natural gift for astronomical
studies. Successful architects; astronomers.

Liver the most sensitive organ.
Hebrew Cabbala
Watery productions of the earth; love of
plants, especially those for curing maladies.
Natural hardihood, and daring; honorable ac-
tions. Favor of persons in authority.

Lowest form: Love of money; resistance;
opposition.
Chinese Tao and Yi-King
Overthrowing or being overthrown. Astronomy. Taciturn. Must not be spasmodic; if he
has faith in a thing all will agree except very
few. Seek to strengthen those below them to

secure place and stability of their own position. Living in retirement. Be sparing of your talk and possess yourself.

24, OR THE LETTER X

Generally fortunate in w o r l d l y affairs. Brought into connection with those in high or influential position. Danger of falls, especially from a horse. Also of illnesses which prevent the use of the legs. Quiet, sincere; one who does not worry greatly, believing that all will be right in the end. Fond of peace. Does not like noise of any kind. Loves music; generally a nice voice of middle register. Artistic talent.

Should not ride horseback, climb, nor go near the edge of high cliffs, nor have much to do with high windows. Danger of injuries to the back.

Should guard the heart.

Hebrew Cabbala

Confers the association of persons in high position and gives success through women of influence. Truthful, sincere.

Lowest form: Discord; quarrels, separation. Exiles, fugitives, prisoners.

Chinese Tao and Yi-King

Does not stand firm. Tends to conceit. Shutting the gates of passes so travelling princes or merchants cannot pursue their occupations. Evil consequent on being all astray because course is not proper to that of a ruler. Trouble from indulgence. Later indicates free course and movements. Movement directed by natural order, or in accordance with order. No one to distress him in his exits and entrances.

25, OR THE LETTER Y

Gives prophetic dreams or strong intuition which amounts at times to having presentiments or second sight. Dominates occult science, wisdom, and talent for penetrating mysteries. Sincerity; will fight crime. Determination, reserve; love of nature. Safe on water; can become expert swimmers. Successful in anything connected with water. The sum of "Annette" is 25, which puts Annette Kellerman under this number.

Spleen most easily affected.

Hebrew Cabbala

For discovering the truth of hidden things. Wisdom. Occult science. Revelations in dreams. High office under protection; success through contact; power acquired by experience; the fruits of action. Messenger.

Lowest form: Developing occult powers for harmful purposes. Worry, confusion.

Chinese Tao and Yi-King

Imagining the mysterious. Sincere. Reaps without having ploughed. Trouble arising from renewed attempts after a thing is finished. Progress but danger of error. Motive power and strength. Causes his family to forget their poverty. Shares with inferiors. His wish is to return to the solitude of his own mind. Minister of communication.

26, OR THE LETTER Z

Repression and therefore a repressed nature; frequently repressed by circumstances as well. It gives, however, as an offset, confidence in self, not egotism, and the power and ability to control others, even, very often, when in a state of violent excitement. This trait may never come to the surface except in emergencies, and the owner may never know that he or she possesses it until occasion arises for its use.

This number is also excellent for secret-service work, or in diplomatic departments. Good writers; energetic; clever speaker; fond of mysteries. In the lower walks of life make successful locksmiths and clock makers. In the underworld make excellent burglars.

Stomach usually the most delicate organ.

Hebrew Cabbala

Influences for politics; diplomats; agents of secret service expeditions. Confidence; security; honor; good faith.

L o w e s t form: Traitors, conspirators; treachery.

Chinese Tao and Yi-King

Concealed enlightenment. External things. That which comes from without. May be good or evil. External advantages or external disadvantages. Quietude and gravity. Accumulation of virtue. Power to keep the strongest in restraint. Strength and solidity. Calmly sits with deliberate mind. If too light will lose his vassals; if too passionate will lose his throne. Stores up words and deeds of former men to subserve this accumulation of virtue.

DEFINITION OF NUMBERS
27

Sometimes gives presentiments. Desires to civilize and nourish, therefore successful in teaching or in business connected with food. It is also a very literary number and its owners often become distinguished in this line.

Genital organs and possibility of digestive troubles.

Hebrew Cabbala

Order, discipline; good arrangement, authority, command; creative intellect; useful works. Dominates propagation of light and civilization. Loves peace, justice, science and art; distinguished in literature.

Lowest form: ignorance, intolerance.

Chinese Tao and Yi-King

Denotes nourishing one's body and mind, one's self or others. Dexterity in using. Skillful at saving men and things without displaying how it is done. Maintains watchfulness over words and is temperate in eating and drinking. Function of skill. Good travelers; good speakers. Applied enlightenment. The bad respect people's wealth. Very spiritual though his knowledge is greatly confused. Examinations, promotions, et cetera.

28

Sometimes brought into connection with fires or explosions, but nearly always comes out safely. Good for getting money and for health. Simplicity, good judgment, originality, inventive ability. Critical, artistic, especially good in designing. Successful leaders, usually become head of a business.

Watch the head and lungs.

Hebrew Cabbala

Protects against fires, explosions, falling walls. Dominates health; simplicity, good judgment. Great dislike to loud, sudden or discordant noises.

Lowest Form: Quarrels, evil associations, discord.

Chinese Tao and Yi-King

Satisfaction and flexibility. Success. Man's strength in female feebleness. Take unwrought material and make it into vessels. Stands up alone and has no fear. Becomes head officer. Evil from boldness but no blame. Covering the body dead or alive. Called to employment. Fond of disgrace or startling unconventionality.

29

Natural reformer. Sometimes very religious, very nervous, and especially particular about certain things. Generous, often extravagant. Rather suspicious of people, or a little distrustful or afraid of them. Fearful of many things. Danger in connection with water; should be very cautious in regard to it; also keep away from heights. Watch the nerves and brain. Successful in business lines. Strong tendency to immorality and dissipation.

Hebrew Cabbala

Indecision, doubt, hesitation, anxiety. Virtue and zeal in propagating the truth. Success, gain, advantage.

Lowest Form: Fanaticism, hypocrisy.

Chinese Tao and Yi-King

All is peril to him and unrest. Covets riches; covets power; may be said to be in a state of disease. Indoors apprehension of thieves; outdoors afraid of being injured. Indoors have many chambers and partitions; outdoors dares not go alone. In a state of constant alarm. Taking no action. Non-assertion. Should he desire to get the kingdom for himself he will not succeed. Practices business of instruction. Misses proper course. Action and advance, achievement. Dangerous heights should not be ascended. (This number does not always bring these extremes, but will do so if not held under control.)

30

Patience and hope. Its owners rarely despair even under great stress. Sees over large spaces mentally and for this reason better in handling large affairs than small ones; for the same reason inclined to exaggerate. Especially good at writing plays, or operas, or in any theatrical line. Very fond of theatres and music. Fine actors. Usually a very fine voice. Apt to be baritone or contralto. Docility. Splendid physicians, surgeons or nurses. Fond of children and animals. Successful in connection with canals and irrigations.

Guard the throat.

Against chagrin and despair; and for having patience. Dominates chemistry, medicine, surgery. Distinguished for anatomy and medicine.

Lowest form: Infidelity, treachery, disloyalty.

Chinese Tao and Yi-King

Perfects and transforms all. Free and successful course. Docility. Fond of fencing and swords. Skillful commander; strikes a decisive blow and stops. Cultivates brilliant virtues and diffuses them over the four quarters. Resolute but not boastful nor haughty; not arrogant nor violent.

31

Liking for astronomy, mathematics, geometry. Succesful nurses, singers, actors, or in mechanical lines. Excellent lawyers. Tends to early marriage. Love for flowers and plants of all kinds. Excitement will upset the circulation of the blood.

Hebrew Cabbala

Dominates vegetation and agriculture. Loves astronomy, mathematics, geometry. Excellent lawyer.

Lowest Form: Avarice, usury; legal proceedings.

Chinese Tao and Yi-King

He who enjoys the slaughter of men will not attain his will in the empire. Uses arms only on compulsion. Calm and repose, are what he prizes. Keeps himself free from preoccupation; open to receive the influences of others' minds on what is beyond himself. Unsettled in his movements. Aim is trivial. Talks with loquacious mouth. Husband and wife. Union, mutually influencing, moving and responding to each other, thereby forcing union. Heaven and earth exert their influences and there ensues the transformation and production of all things. Marriage.

32

Represents "long enduring" and therefore gives long life. Good memory, love of social life; many friends. Brought into contact with m a n y people. Successful in languages, or writing or whatever power of endurance, or an especially good memory would be useful.

Guard the liver.

Hebrew Cabbala

Dominates justice; good memory. Society; union, association, concord, harmony; ease of speech.

Lowest Form: Bad qualities of body and soul.

Chinese Tao and Yi-King

Long continuance; docility and motive force. Advantage comes from long continued operations. Denotes long endurance. Sweet dew of Heaven and earth which reaches equally everywhere. Men rest in it without error or risk of failure. Stands firm, does not change his method. Long continuance without special effort. Mixed experiences without weariness. Uniformity of virtue. Men flock to it; cannot be kept away.

33

Musicians, actors, clergymen, artists, physicians, nurses, bird-fanciers. Strong instinct for protecting others. Desire to get away from crowded places and live near to nature. Happier and more successful when away from cities. Usually fortunate financially.

Watch throat and heart.

Hebrew Cabbala

Musicians, physicians, surgeons. Commerce; trade, new enterprises.

Lowest Form: Encourage revolts.

Chinese Tao and Yi-King

Business has its regular course. Clothes and food are provided for. Stores are filled. Cattle are fattened and looked after. Old and weak, orphans and solitary receive anxious consideration. In all these ways provision is made. Denotes withdrawing under Heaven or Sky. Successful progress from retiring. Discrimination. Knows other men and himself. Overcomes others and himself. Is satisfied with his lot. Acts with energy. Keep small men at a distance by his own dignified gravity. Retires in a noble manner which will be advantageous in all ways.

34

Strong religious feeling; good temper; talent. Strength and vigor; good leadership. Does not like change. Power to achieve. Determination in overcoming obstacles.

Bilious troubles.

Hebrew Cabbala

Against choler. Celebrated for their talents and actions; confidence and fervor of prayers. Success. Many surprises and strange occurrences.

Lowest Form: Discord, treachery.

Chinese Tao and Yi-King

Does not claim the honor of having done but quietly accomplishes. Task of achievement. All pervading. Does not take a step which is not in accordance with propriety. Too much attention to propriety makes one unable to advance or retreat. If he realizes this there will be good fortune. Strength directing movement and vigor.

35

Very faithful to a trust. Usually a sunny, hopeful temperament; very friendly. Apt to remain in one place a long time. If possible, like to keep the same persons in his employment, and anxious to reward faithful service. Usually inherits money; often through the friendliness of others. Successful writers, speakers, architects. Generally considerable travel. Digestive troubles at times.

Hebrew Cabbala

Dominates testaments, successions, g i f t s, legacies given through friendless. Loves to live in peace with all the world and to recompense the fidelity of those who serve him.

Lowest Form: Cruelty, tyranny, persecution, violence.

Chinese Tao and Yi-King

Attribute of benevolence. Docile submission. A Prince who secures the tranquility of the people, and is presented with numerous horses by the King. Men resort to him to find rest, peace, and a feeling of ease. Entertains with music and dainties. Wishes to advance; pursues correct course all alone. Will receive official charge. All trust him. Need not worry whether he succeeds or fails, course will bring congratulations; will advance.

36

Quiet, amiable, serious; careful of their possesions. Stand in their own light. Injure themselves by well-intentioned but misguided actions, which lead to the destruction of perhaps the very thing most deired. When this occurs he will, if at all possible, rush to his home for sympathy. Very peculiar about eating. Usually fine voices.

Digestion and genital organs.

Hebrew Cabbala

For maintaining the position where one is employed, and preserving the means which one possesses. Goodness, kindness, liberality, generosity.

Lowest Form: Shifty in his dealings. Distrust, doubt, suspicion. Losing positions, deceit.

Chinese Tao and Yi-King

Hiding the light from yourself. Raised up then thrown down. Given gifts then despoiled. Shows intelligence by keeping it obscured. At first ascended to the top of the sky. Might have enlightened the four quarters. End will be to go into the ground; has failed to fulfill the model of a ruler. The secret explanation. Brightness wounded or obscured; accomplished and bright; pliant and submissive. Advantageous to realize the difference of the position and obscure one's brightness. Wounded. He who is wounded abroad will return to his home.

37

Great love for money and show, with a strong desire to rule. Very contrary, especially upsetting in family life. A desire to dictate is often its undoing. All the quick traits of the 10, but not as good a leader, as it sees only its own way which is usually the wrong one. When this number occurs in either sex a partner who is entirely willing to submit to the rule of the other, should be carefully selected in marriage.

Danger to head and lungs.

Hebrew Cabbala

Dominates science and art. Inspires philosophers, sages, distinguished savants. Perverse spirit. Union, marriage, protection and success through women of high position. Also success through association with opposite sex. Good will; friendship.

Lowest form: Intermeddling and to be distrusted.

Chinese Tao and Yi-King

Authoritative ruler. Exercise of government. Should speak according to truth and make his conduct consistent. Shows his true character, display of majesty.

When the right administration of the family is at an end, misunderstanding and division will come. Let father be father, and son, son. The man and woman should occupy their correct places. Family is enriched.

38

Literary fame. Sometime creates misunderstandings and quarrels. Religious, generous; possibly extravagant. Apt to have many difficulties. Nerves.

Hebrew Cabbala

Dominates those who are in rapport with God. Can acquire much treasure both earthly and spiritual.

Lowest form: Hypocrisy, falseness, lies, fraud, cunning; abuse of confidence.

Chinese Tao and Yi-King

Two living together whose wills do not move in the same direction. Denotes misunderstanding and division; sure to give rise to complications and difficulties. Where there is general agreement admits diversity of opinion. Leads to harmonious agreement and the passing away of all doubts. Should have everything solid and nothing flimsy. Bright intelligence. Traditionalism. Great organizer.

39

Usually good health and long life; strong paternal and filial love. Many difficulties. Should live in the southwest; southwest corner of a street; room or house should face southwest. Can become very cruel.

Guard the throat. Excellent physician.

Hebrew Cabbala

Dominates health and long life. Paternal and filial love. For the curing of maladies.

Lowest form: The greatest cruelty known. Infanticide, parricide.

Chinese Tao and Yi-King

If haughty, their fall is imminent. Dignity. Low position, or those who raise themselves from low position. Should examine himself and cultivate virtue. Struggle with great difficulties. Peril in front. Advantage in the southwest. No advantage in the northeast.

40

Careful with money though fond of investing it. Frequently connected with printing and libraries. Literary lines, and art. Also successful in business and mechanical lines. Love of travel, especially by water. Has a temper.

Circulation of the blood.

Hebrew Cabbala

Men of letters and artists. Dominates printing and libraries. Honor, confidence, consideration. Sometimes a tendency to sombre spirits
and shunning society.

Lowest form: Strife, opposition, differences,
disputes.

Chinese Tao and Yi-King

Escape from peril; advantage in the southwest.

The movement will win all. Successful operations. Buds of plants and trees begin to burst
and produce fruit. Denotes relaxation and ease.
Forgives errors and deals gently with others.
Removes rebellion.

41

Religious. Energy. Versatility. Fine speakers
and writers. Control of the temper and the passions. Successful in politics and literary lines.

Trouble with liver.

Hebrew Cabbala

Energy. Occupied with political affairs.
Heads of diplomats.

Lowest form: Apostates, renegades.

Chinee Tao and Yi-King

Restrains wrath; represses desire. Diminishes
the ailment under which he labors. Gives to
others without decreasing his own. Obtains
his wish on a grand scale. Cultivation of virtue.
Difficulty in the beginning, but ease in the end.
Keeping what is harmful at a distance.

42

Religious. Often clergymen. Musical talent. Quiet, calm, artists, singers.

The Heart; good for marriage, but not especially good for health.

Hebrew Cabbala

Grandeur of soul. Energy. Consecrated to the services of God. Dominates religion.

Lowest form: Traitors.

Chinese Tao and Yi-King

Diminution and increase. Overflowing and emptiness. Should be employed in sacrifice. The violent or strong do not die a natural death.

43

Displacing or removing; love for military life, though danger in war or from firearms for this particular number.

Bilious troubles.

Hebrew Cabbala

Love, glory and the military state. Many projects.

Lowest form: Discord; revolution.

Chinese Tao and Yi-King

Overcomes by softness. Advantage in non-action. Bestows emoluments on those below him. Is not in the place appropriate to him. Misery in having none on whom to call. Written characters and bonds. Offices regulated and people accurately examined. Displacing or removing. Danger from war or arms. For making one's name known.

44

Success in useful enterprises. Dominates voyages, especially those made for instruction. Love for military life. Brave; may win military distinction.

Circulation of the blood and stomach.

Hebrew Cabbala

Success in useful e n t e r p r i s e ; and distinguished for military talent and bravery; becomes celebrated within the records of glory.

Lowest form: Domineering; war; revolution. Imagining one's self distinguished.

Chinese Tao and Yi-King

Seeks fame and riches to his own detriment. Delivers his charges; promulgates his announcements throughout the four quarters. Keeps himself too much aloof from people. Exhausted at his greatest height. Self-restraint. Excessive love of name will be attended with much personal sacrifice. Excessive hoarding will be followed by great ruin. If one knows where to stop there is no danger.

(It will be seen that the dominant tendency of this number is to make its owner distinguished. As examples, we give Andrew *Carnegie, Gertrude* Atherton, *Gertrude* Vanderbilt (Mrs. Harry Payne Whitney), Thomas *Jefferson*.)

45

Dominates love of instructing; facility in learning; vegetation. Union. Often early marriage. Successful teachers, in leading multitudes or in anything connected with many people.

Genital organs and stomach.

Hebrew Cabbala

For confounding wickedness and arrogance and relieving those who are humiliated and declining. Dominates vegetation; love of instructing; learns with facility. Union; marriage.

Lowest form: Revolution, false projects.

Chinese Tao and Yi-King

Great or overflowing v i r t u e. Puts the weapons of war in good repair to be prepared against contingencies.

Ex-President *Theodore* Roosevelt was a striking example of this as witnessed by his work for preparedness during the World War.

46

Very high ideals. Steady upward advancement. Flexibility; obedience. Successful with those in power. Psychic number, which has strong intuition, often amounting to presentiments. Fortitude; discretion. Should live in the south. Sometimes make great discoveries. Must guard the lungs.

Usually acquires money but generally loses it through sacrificing it to high ideals.

Hebrew Cabbala

Power to see in dreams. Discovers secrets of nature. Fortitude; subtle ideas; new and sublime thoughts; discretion.

Lowest form: Ennui; displeasure; discon-

tent; dissatisfaction.
Chinese Tao and Yi-King

Moderating of desire or ambition. When this prevails at its best, the swift horses draw dung carts (agriculture) when disregarded they breed war horses. The fault is to sanction ambition and desire to get. When correct, develops virtue until high and great. Succeeds in his aim but will not preserve his riches.

47

Agreeable. Most successful line is handling money for, or through, the people. Philosophical. Excellent bankers and brokers. Danger from water and multitudes of people.

Nerves.
Hebrew Cabbala

Dominates justice. Agreeable character. Passion for acquiring the secrets of light, in a material as well as a mental sense. Quick, especially in business; celerity; vigilance. Usually successful.

Lowest form: Immoral actions; scandal.
Chinese Tao and Yi-King

Should not make speeches, argue nor plead. Surveying what is far off. Without going out the door one understands all that takes place. The farther one goes out the less he knows. Accomplish their purpose without really intending to do so. Extreme difficulty ending in free course. Exercise of discrimination; diminution of resentment. Surveying what is far off. Viewing the distant.

48

Affectionate nature, very fond of pleasure.
Psychic; sometimes has prophetic dreams or
presentiments. Faithful in partnerships and
marriage. Sometimes difficulty in finishing
undertakings. Success in lines connected with
entertainments and amusemets.

The throat.

Hebrew Cabbala

Love; friendship; sincerity; affection. Tries
to preserve the union between husband and wife.
Gives presentiments and secret inspirations.
Passion for love. Fond of pleasure.

Lowest form: Inconstancy: too great love
of luxury.

Chinese Tao and Yi-King

Well, which supplies nourishment and is not
exhausted. Returning to the ground. Forgetting
knowledge. Takes the empire by using no diplomacy. Increases his knowledge and decreases
his doing until he does nothing on purpose.
Having arrived at non-action there is nothing
he does not do. He gets as his own all under
heaven by doing nothing. If he takes trouble
he will not get it. Comforts the people. Stimu-
lates the people to mutual helpfulness. The
grand accomplishment takes place.

49

Sensible and generous. Love of law and

literature. Absolutely universal. Diplomatic. Many changes but nearly always for the better. Tends to feasts and banquets.

Circulation of the blood.

Hebrew Cabbala

Feasting; banquets; good cheer. Sensible and generous. Love literature; jurisprudence. Diplomat. Spiritual mind; change; novelty.

Lowest form: Egotism; hatred; hypocrisy.

Chinese Tao and Yi-King

Trust in virtue; anxious in his dealings with the world. Universalizes his heart and the hundred families fix upon him their eyes and ears. Treats them all like children. The quality of indulgence. Free from preoccupation therefore ready for all. Amelioration. Heart not set on anything; no fixed opinions; accomodates to the minds of others; thus becomes a saviour. Change. Cultivated intelligence; satisfaction believed in after change is accomplished.

50

Like the 49 tends to feasts and banquets. Dominates justice; lawyers; advocates. Eloquent speakers; pleaders at the bar; in public meetings, etc. A person of many affairs. Fine sight and hearing; usually very brilliant eyes.

Sight and liver.

Hebrew Cabbala

A lawyer; a man of law; power; command; superiority; authority. Dominates justice; advocates. Industrious and active; a person of many affairs. Loves literature and is distinguished for eloquence.

Lowest form: Wickedness; disturbance.
Chinese Tao and Yi-King

The great man arouses himself to his work. Apt to live a life of too intensified activity. Luxurious. Opulent. Maintains secure the appointments of heaven. Estimation of life. Need not fear fierce animals; need not fear arms; does not belong to the realm of death. Cooking; feasts; flexible obedience; ears quick of hearing; eyes clear sighted. Great progress and success.

51

Talent for chemistry, physics, medicine, abstract science. Can become distinguished physicians and surgeons. Easily filled with apprehension and dread, yet smiles and talks cheerfully. Movement and change. Generally successful in spite of fears. Love of music, usually good voice. Very quiet. Talent for languages. Gives strange occurrences.

Physically indicates the heart.
Hebrew Cabbala

Dominates chemistry and physics. Universal medicine. Loves abstract science, distinguished in medicine. Conditions often arise which prevent marriage or bring about absence or separation after marriage. Often abundance which is accompanied with much worry.

Lowest form: Ill-temper and much fear.
Chinese Tao and Yi-King

The operation of nourishing things. Quiet and passionless. Examines his faults. Walks amid startling movement but successful. Ease and development. Looks out with apprehension, but feeling of dread leads to happiness. In spite of fears, smiles and talks cheerfully. Startling occurrences.

52

Usually many voyages. Strong and vigorous temperament. Supports adversity with prudence and courage. Loves to work, skillful, able, prompt. Fondness for the military. Determination. Love of mountains.

The spleen.

Hebrew Cabbala

Dominates soldiers and voyages. Temperament strong and vigorous. Supports adversity with patience and courage. Loves to work. Skillful, prompt.

Lowest form: Very conceited.

Chinese Tao and Yi-King

Generous and good. Close the lips and eyes and as long as you live you will have no trouble, but open the lips and meddle and you will never be out of trouble. The desire is to close one's door and be quiet. Should remain unagitated.

53

Very serious temperament. Fond of meditation. Given to carefully overlooking and matching every detail of any matter. Splendid scouts in military work. Excellent detectives.

Steady advancement. Quiet. Sometimes descends to stealthiness and spying.

Possible stomach and throat troubles.

Hebrew Cabbala

Melancholy humor. Loves repose and meditation. Liking for abstract science. Authority. Overlooking.

Lowest form: A spy.

Chinese Tao and Yi-King

Restfulness, flexibility; penetration; advance; increase of evidence. Gaining insight. Afraid of expansion.

54

Eloquence. Fine writers and orators. Often wins reputation as a savant. Usually long life. Apt to bring difficulties.

Physically governs the genital organs.

Hebrew Cabbala

Celebrated for writing and eloquence; good reputation among savants.

Lowest form: Ruin of governments.

Chinese Tao and Yi-King

Cultivating and observing. Vigor; riches; far-seeing. Danger of becoming lame.

55

Moral and high-minded. Generally noted for good deeds and qualities. Honest and honorable. Frequently become clergymen or belong to religious orders. Bright and intelligent. Usually fortunate in money matters. Danger of breaking the right arm. Generally strong voice.

Physically indicates the head and liver.

Hebrew Cabbala

Dominates morals and religion. Distinguished for faith and piety. An ecclesiastic.

Lowest form: Enemies of virtue.

Chinese Tao and Yi-King

Intelligence and movement directed by intelligence. It is for him to cause his light to shine on all under the sky. The mysterious charm. Harmony. Poisonous insects cannot sting him. No danger from ugly animals. Firm grasp; strong throat and voice. Keeps himself withdrawn from others but has large house. Breaks right arm. Full of life and vitality.

56

Frequently brings renown and fortune. Philosophical, modest, agreeable. Frequent changes of environment. Apt to retire into the background and have only few selected friends.

Must guard the nerves.

Hebrew Cabbala

Esteemed by all for modesty and agreeable humor. Dominates renown, fortune and philosophy.

Lowest form: Too great ambition.

Chinese Tao and Yi-King

To blunt sharp angles, unravel disorder, soften the glare. The mysterious excellence. Does not talk much. Has the means of livelihood but uneasy mind. Reaches high place.

57

Success in commerce. Brave, frank, affectionate, sweet nature.

Watch the throat.

Hebrew Cabbala

Prosperity. L o v e for the military; distinguished for activity and for supporting fa-
tigue with good courage.

Lowest form: Treachery.

Chinese Tao and Yi-King

Genuineness. Make the upright rule the
nation. Advancing and receding. Tries too
hard to penetrate; becomes exhausted.

58

Good nature and usually good health. Brave,
frank, affectionate. Successful in commerce or
as a physician; especially as an eye specialist.

Watch the eyes and sight.

Hebrew Cabbala

For curing maladies; especially those of the
eyes. Brave, frank, many love affairs.

Lowest form: Choler; wickedness; homicide.

Chinese Tao and Yi-King

Straightforward, but without license. Bright
but does not dazzle. Pleasure in leading and
attracting others.

59

Success with boats and shipping.

S t r o n g love for speculation and even
gambling. Considerable travel by water. Natural bankers and brokers. Apt to be connected

with libraries and printing. Apt to give liver troubles.

Hebrew Cabbala

Dominates treasure, banks, stocks, printing, libraries.

Lowest form: Gambling; fraudulent failures; swindling.

Chinese Tao and Yi-King

Rides in vessel over water and will do so to advantage. Conquers every obstacle. Lives long and sees many days. Power long to observe the affairs of this world. Return to normal, subjugation of every obstacle to this end. Scatters making good fortune. May be ruler of the state. Far removed from danger of injury.

60

Fastidious; usually long life. Given to making many rules and regulations. Execllent lawyers, superintendents, managers.

Cheerfulness. Excellent nurses or companions for those inclined to despondency.

Watch the heart.

Hebrew Cabbala

For the curing of maladies of the spirit. Fastidious; long life. Regulations.

Lowest form: Insubordination.

Chinese Tao and Yi-King

Regulation. Controlled by authority in its proper place. If too severe will come to an end.

61

Sensible; sincere. Will win the confidence of the people. Love of travel and of all honest pleasure.

Apt to give bilious attacks.

Hebrew Cabbala

Love voyages and all honest pleasures. Sensible mind.

Lowest form: Misrule, quarrels.

Chinese Tao and Yi-King

Sincerity. Humility; condescends to the small states, so gains them all. Conquering by quietness.

62

Fond of regulations. Love of detail, so will usually succeed in any work requiring detail, or in connection with small articles. Excellent chemists or druggists. Must not go to high places.

May suffer from indigestion or other stomach troubles.

Hebrew Cabbala

For acquiring wisdom. Dominates philosophy. Loves tranquility and solitude. Modesty; virtue.

Lowest form: Inconstancy and divorce.

Chinese Tao and Yi-King

Exceeding in small things or affairs. Must not undertake large ones. To ascend is contrary to reason; to descend is natural and right. Admirable deeds raise them above others. Admirable words purchase honor. Exceeds proper course; indicates habit of domineering.

63

Natural reformer. Good missionaries. Generally good health. Usually safe from accidents. Subtle and ingenious, industrious and active. Successful in commerce, banking, or as a physician.

Physically indicates the genital organs.

Hebrew Cabbala

For converting the nations. Protects from accidents, cures maladies. Dominates commerce and bankers. Subtle and ingenious, industrious and active.

Lowest form: Folly; a prodigal.

Chinese Tao and Yi-King

Progress and success in small matters for a time but usually ends in a cessation of effort; then disorder arises. Thinking in the beginning.

Head immersed, position perilous.

64

Good temper. Successful as professors, orators, or in literary lines. Tends to remain single.

Watch the lungs and breath organs.

Hebrew Cabbala

Protects from anger and ferocious animals. Dominates professors, orators, and those distinguished in literature.

Lowest form: False savants; over-critical.

Chinese Tao and Yi-King

Guarding the minute. Learns what others

disregard. Returns and gathers what others pass. Does not know how to submit to the proper regulations.

CHAPTER IV

MANNER OF ARRANGING TABLES FOR READING
PAST, PRESENT AND FUTURE
EVENTS IN LIFE

THE reading of events in the life is the most difficult part of Name Analyzation, as it depends greatly on careful and skilled judgment as well as expert knowledge of the subject.

We give here merely a statement of *facts* as they exist in this science, and make no attempt in this brief work to offer explanations concerning them, or reasons for their being.

A few experiments in any of the lines embraced in this book will abolutely corroborate in every way the accuracy of the statements made.

We pass through each name, by vibration, in the exact amount of years, as the whole number to which each *name* adds; remaining in each letter, likewise the same amount of years as the number to which that letter corresponds in the table.

For instance, taking the name *Mary. The owner* will remain in the *M* four years; in the *A* one year; in the *R* nine years, and in the *Y* seven; making in all the sum of twenty-one years. In other words, she will be twenty-one years of age when she has completed the name for the first time. She will then *begin the name over again,* and be forty-two years old when she has completed it for the second time. This repeats, in this manner, throughout the life depending for the number of times upon the *length* of the name.

The same action is taking place in regard to the middle and surname, as well as in connection with the mother's maiden name.

For example, we will suppose the name to be *Mary Grace Smith,* and the maiden name of the mother to have been *Clarkson.* Mary Smith would, of course, begin life in the *initial* letters of all the names. She would therefore, be *four* years of age when she passed from the *M* to the *A* of Mary. She would remain there —in the *A* vibration—*one* year, and would be *five* years of age when she passed from the *A* to the *R;* this letter covers a period of *nine* years. Her age, therefore, when she passed to the *Y,* would be fourteen years. The *Y* occupies seven more years; thus she would have reached the age of twenty-one years. She would then return to the *M,* remaining in it as before, four years; this would bring her to twenty-five years of age; the *A* is again one year, making the age twenty-six. The nine years of the *R* carry the age to thirty-five years; and the seven years of the *Y* reach to the forty-second year, when returning for the third time to the *M,* she would begin as before. The same thing is occurring with the other names. She remains in the *G* of *Grace* until her seventh year, in the *R* nine more, making her sixteen years of age when she passes to the *A*, seventeen when the *C* is reached, twenty when the *E* is begun, and twenty-five when the name is ended. She then returns to the *G*, et cetera.

Therefore the tables for the events belonging to this name would stand as follows:

M A R Y	G R A C E	S M I T H
4 5 14 21	7 16 17 20 25	1 5 14 16 24
25 26 35 42	32 41 42 45 50	25 29 38 40 48
46 47 56 63 etc.	57 66 etc.	49 53 62 64 etc.

C L A R K S O N
3 6 7 16 18 19 25 30
33 36 37 46 48 49 55 60
63 etc.

It must be distinctly remembered that the numbers placed under the letters represent the age reached when that particular letter has terminated, or is just *terminating*, its own especial action for the time.

We will now place these letters together in the manner in which they will be acting in the life.

One year being the age in this case at which the first change took place, we begin there. At that age, then, this child was in the following tables:

The M of Mary

G of Grace

Changing from S to m of Smith

C of Clarkson

The next change marked is at four years; and the table then stands:

Changing from the M to a in Mary

In ”   G of Grace

”   ”   m of Smith

”   ”   C of Clarkson

The next age marked is at the fifth year; and here it must be noticed that at this time a change is taking place in two names; therefore it will be a more important event on this account. The table thus stands:

Changing from the a to r of Mary

In G of Grace

Changing from the m to i in Smith

C of Clarkson

Sufficient explanation has now been given to enable anyone to understand the method by which these tables are formed.

An examination of the further tables of this name shows that at twenty-five there is a change taking place in all four names. Whenever this occurs it will be found to be an event of great importance in the life.

A few tables will be given showing the manner in which they are read. The rest must be left to the study and skill of the student.

We have before stated that when more *B's* than one are present particularly as initials, they are apt to give delicacy of health, sometimes permanently, but in any case during such periods as they may get together in the vibration. Therefore a table which reads

B
B
L

would mean greatly delicacy of health for a period covering from two to three years.

As *L* governs the throat, it would further show that the trouble was connected with that organ. These being all initials would have a stronger influence than those in other positions. The child of course began life with them—they include the first name, surname, and mother's maiden name—and as *B* covers a period of two years and *L* three, the child suffered with serious bronchial trouble during the first two years of its existence. Whether it would recover or not depended largely upon the letters to which it was changing at the age of two. In this case it changed from one *B* to an *L* and from the other *B* to an *R*. That placed the table

B to L
. L
B to R

Therefore both of the letters which were causing the trouble dropped out at this time.

The second *L* acted further upon the throat, giving it more strength, while the *R*, which tends to strengthen the entire body, aided in the efforts of the second *L* and brought about recovery.

Suppose, however, there had been a fourth letter in the table, and it had been an *M*, as the strongest quality of that letter is its constant action of creation and destruction; it would probably have ended in the child's death, or at the very least, a terribly hard struggle for life. Had it been changing to more than one *M*, its death would have been practically a certainty. Had the letter, on the other hand, been a *C, K, G*, or any other of those which are protective or vivifying forces, it would generally mean recovery.

This, however, is not intended to convey the idea that an *M* in a table always indicates a death; *two* usually do so, but often that of a relative. It frequently indicates travel; and if the rest of the table be good it may be a very pleasant period.

Those having many *N's* in their names nearly always marry young, or at least have opportunities to do so. When there is an *N* in a name it is usually present in the table meaning marriage. For example, one marriage table reads:

n

E to L

e

n to g

The capital letter indicates an initial. The *N's* as just stated, nearly always indicate marriage, or at least an opportunity in that line. The *E's* gives eventfulness, or, rather, eventful action to the rest of the letters. The l to which one of the *E's* was changing, gives expansion and possession. One *n* is changing to a *g*; and this nearly always indicates gain of some sort. This table, therefore, gives an almost certain marriage. However, there are innumerable other tables which also give marriages, deaths, etc., as death tables must *always* occur; and marriage tables *nearly* always, no matter what the combination of letters may be. It is easy to see that happy events might be frequently brought about by some names, while unhappy ones might be almost entirely the fate of others.

It is the fact that *much* of this unhappiness is utterly unnecessary and that the science of Name Analyzation gives the knowledge which will provide for its prevention, which renders it of such grave importance to humanity.

As it is impossible to enumerate the endless tables which occur in the equally endless combinations of names; and as their correct interpretation *must* depend in any case upon the practice and skill of the student, the only thing which can be done in a work of this kind is to give the most important underlying principles.

CHAPTER V

JUDGING THE EVENTS

THIS part of Name Analyzation is the most difficult part of the science and requires great care and practice; nevertheless it more than repays all the labor which may be bestowed upon it as it is extremely accurate as to past, present and future.

In reading the events from the table of letters produced by the methods described in the last chapter, we use principally those portions of the definitions of the letters and numbers which relate to the fortune and circumstances; the general characteristics of these also have to be taken into consideration, so it is of the utmost importance to be thoroughly familiar with the action of each separate letter.

It must be thoroughly understood that the definitions given here are the *general* tendencies of the *letters* when entirely apart from their *individualized* meanings according to the *different periods of birth*.

The use of these various periods of birth in connection with the Chinese *Circle of Heaven* are taken up in the more advanced study of the Yi-King, Tao as well as the good and bad combinations of letters.

A name containing many of the letter *a*, such as *Barbara*, will always produce an active, generally a *very* active person. A in a table of events, will always produce activity in *all* the other letters which constitute the table. If therefore, the events indicated are good ones, the *a* renders them more active in a fortunate direction; in the same manner, if evil, the *a* will assist in throwing them to the evil side. Its period of vibration is one year.

B indicates a spiritual condition of mind and body. It produces a highly strung period, and therefore, to a certain extent, physical delicacy during its vibration, which covers two years. Two of these letters in a table are almost certain to indicate danger to the health and, sometimes the brain. It occurs sometimes in marriage tables, and in such a case indicates that the person will marry with rather high ideals.

C is a vivifying force, and therefore tends to produce physically a much healthier condition of mind and body. As however, it indicates the throat in a bad table, it might produce trouble in this direction. In the circumstances of the life it is apt to show difficulty in advancing, and the possibility of having to humble one's self to those beneath one to gain the thing desired. Its vibration covers three years.

D produces movement of a decided character. One usually indicates travel, generally of a pleasant nature, though this depends upon the *entire* table; that is, whether the other letters are fortunate or otherwise. It further shows that the person will be placed in some position giving him or her greater authority and power. Two of these letters in a table are very dangerous, often indicating death. A table reading

L
L
D
D

would almost surely mean death by an accident. One reading

N
N
D
D

would mean a very dangerous illness or death through an accident, and unless the name were changed in time—almost certain death. Its period of vibration is four years.

E adds eventfulness to either good or bad conditions, as indicated by the rest of the table. It makes bad *worse,* and good *better.* In other words it tends to produce more *exciting* reasons for whatever the life table shows at this time. Its vibration acts for five years.

F tends to affect the heart, in a table of illness, such as

F
N
D
N

it would mean either heart trouble or a nervous or weak condition of the heart produced by illness. It also means concealment, and affects material matters for good or bad. If a table read

F

U

O

it would mean financial loss. Its vibration is six years.

G in a table usually indicates gain; if in an illness, it tends to assist in bringing about recovery. If in a marriage table, the marriage is generally almost certain, and the person *tends* to gain in position. With an *f* it tends to financial or business gain. Its period of vibration is seven years.

H represents personal strain; if with a *g*, it will be strain either for pleasure or gain, which will be successful. If with a *u*, it will be produced by loss, and therefore necessity. If with an *o*, strain in regard to money. If with an *n*, strain producing great nervous effort and perhaps illness. If the table should read

H

D

D

I

it would indicate generally the death of a near

relative, where the personal feelings were strongly involved and nervous strain mentally and physically the result. Its vibratory period is eight years.

I always indicates the *personal* feelings, an extremely sensitive condition which renders the feelings exaggeratedly sharp and therefore tends to produce suffering. It often occurs in tables indicating the death of relatives, also in marriage tables or in those bringing either suffering or pleasure. It makes the person either shy or the exact reverse, bold and aggressive, but in either case sympathetic and intuitive. Its period is nine years.

J will place the person in a position of leadership, willingly or unwillingly. If in business, elevation from something lower; if connected with death, leadership in family affairs. It nearly always means gain and advantage to the person in some form, unless in a very bad table; in this case it would show unwilling leadership under many difficulties. Its period of vibration is one year.

K, while it indicates nervousness, is nevertheless a vivifying force. It gives strength and endurance, and in a table of illness nearly always shows recovery. Its most usual meaning, however, is travel or change. In finance or business, in connection with bad letters, such as *u,* it will be a strong indication of loss, as its tendency is to scatter. It will, on the other hand, in a good table show enlargement of business

K: BAD

or plans of this kind. Success in bold undertakings, though also possible rashness. Its
period is two years.

L produces travel, short or long journeys,
change and movement; but usually much self-
sacrifice. Two in a table are not good; as they
tend to accidents and possibly violent death. If
two appear in a table, or if the vibration is
passing between *a double* l—l to l—there is
especial danger of falling downstairs. The
author personally knows of several cases where
this has occurred. In two instances the person
was killed outright. The vibration of this letter
is three years.

M is another letter of which *more* than one
is dangerous. It produces change, therefore,
one may only indicate travel; but any *violent*
action or change is never good, as it is always
more or less dangerous. As has been constantly
reiterated, *two* of *any* letter *doubles its effect;*
therefore two *M's* produce violent change, thus
often indicating a death. Its period is four
years.

N indicates the *physical* body of the person
to whom the table belongs. One is nearly always an indication of marriage, or an opportunity in this direction. With a *g*, it will be
almost certain, and also an advantageous one.
With a *u*, it will probably come to nothing; with
a *t*, which indicates change of home, it is almost
certain to take place, but if it be with two *t's*
it may indicate brain fever, or brain trouble of

some sort. The same, when the table reads with two *n's* and one *t* or *b*. Two *n's* are almost sure to produce illness when together in a table. Its vibratory action covers five years.

O usually indicates good or bad in financial matters. With a *g* gain; with a *u,* loss; with one *d,* financial matters connected with travel etc., two tend to produce illness which might weaken the heart. Its tendency is to slowness. Its period is six years.

P, unless in a very fortunate name, will usually bring power and success, but ruin often follows in its wake, and when this occurs brain trouble is usually produced also. If *p* occurs with *g,* this will usually result in gain in power; but with *u* it is almost certain ruin, and with *t* or *b,* almost equally certain brain trouble. Its period is seven years.

Q, is good for business, travel and health; it is life-giving, therefore, in a table of illness will strongly tend to produce recovery. In business it is gain; in a marriage table it indicates successful marriage. Its period is eight years.

R gives too great rapidity of action; therefore in most cases it is not good. In a *good* table it is not harmful unless two are present. It represents the material body, so inclines to bring illness and accidents. It has a strong tendency to react on the home, and break it up or bring many domestic worries and cares. It is especially bad for the father when in a bad table. Its period is nine years.

S sharpens but is also tending to protect. It may sharpen an illness, but inclines to bring recovery; it may sharpen trouble of any sort, but helps, at the same time to reduce it. In this manner it also makes *good* better. Its period is one year.

T, usually indicates change of home; *generally* a change for the better, though this, as in all other cases, is influenced by the remainder of the table.

T is often in marriage tables. Its period is two years.

U is almost invariably loss. Its period is three years. BAD ᵞ

V usually indicates travel. If with u, it may BAD 𝒴 show money loses, possibly through speculation or gambling. Two would probably mean loss of, or at least an extravagant spending of, money. Would tend to weakness of character at such a period and probably dissipation. It covers four years.

W produces wavering conditions. In a good table this letter will indicate travel, but as a general thing it is not good. Its action covers five years.

X, of course, rarely occurs in a table; and contains great danger of falls and injury from horses, vehicles, or trains, and great care must be exercised in all these directions during its period of vibration which is six years.

Y will generally give safety on water, and is also good for health in a table of illness. It tends to give success during the period of its action, which is seven years.

Z, controls and represses; therefore tends to recovery in illness. It is sometimes in marriage tables. It may place one in a position where one is controlling or superintending others; or in secret missions. Its period is eight years.

CHAPTER VI

The Connection of Names With the Elements and their Action Upon Physical and Mental Life

EACH portion of the body, however minute, is under the influence of some force already in existence, among the millions of outside forces controlling our lives and the planet upon which we live.

Every action, condition, feeling or emotion occurring in a human body can therefore be translated into a number. Let us reiterate here, however, that *numbers* are not *forces;* they are *symbols* which we use as our guides.

Every atmospheric condition of the earth has also its own minute number, therefore, naturally, so has each season.

To understand this fully we must begin by realizing that *we* are a part of the universe. Each action of the world of Nature, no matter what it is, is taking place in our own bodies in exactly the same form in which it occurs in the world outside.

Each year is but the representation of a day, —in a little longer form.

Spring is the early morning of the year; it is starting the action of the coming Year-Day

DIAGRAM OF THE YIN AND YANG

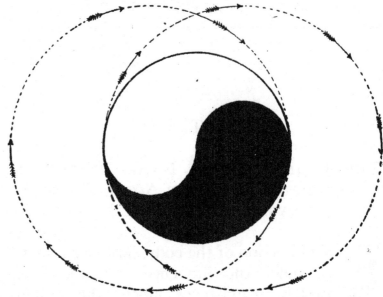

THE above diagram represents the Chinese YIN and YANG, the two great fundamental principles of creative action. YANG is Positive, YIN is Negative; Yang is Heaven, Yin is Earth; Yang is Masculine, Yin is Feminine. Yang is Day, Yin is Night. Yang is the Sun, Yin is the Moon. Yang is everything in creative action which is positive; Yin is everything in creative action which is negative.

The figure wll be easily recognized as one which is frequently seen in different connections. It is always, however, shown in quiescence. No diagram of the YIN and YANG in action has ever before been presented to the Western world. The YANG is White; the YIN is Black. White, therefore, is positive; Black is negative. Each of the comma-like figures has, as will be noticed, a pivot. The white, positive YANG has a black, negative pivot; and the black, negative YIN has a white, positive pivot typifying the constant and actual interchange of the positive and negative forces in the action of the Universe. The Chinese say that the YANG starts whirling on its pivot, then stops; then the YIN whirls on its pivot, and stops, continuing this action constantly and alternately, eternally. Of course it is understood that this action is inconceivably rapid. The reader will at once recognize that the alternating current of positive and negative electricity is distinctly and unquestionably expressed, and the action, as given in the diagram, distinctly portrays the interlocking spirals of opposite motion. Anyone who has any knowledge of the actual winding of an electric dynamo "core" will know at once that *this* is positive fact; the "core" is wound with two wires, the positive and negative, or Male and Female wires, as they are called; one wound to the right and the other to the left. If this were not done, there would be no electric light, or electric action of any sort whatever. With the Chinese the YIN and YANG represents everything from the molecule to the unknowable GOD.

just as we are beginning our own day when we arise in its morning.

The first business of each season is to broadcast its arrival to the waiting Earth.

The radios that have become a part of the furniture of our home are still new to most of us, but the radio sets which are part of each *season's* luggage, are the same ones which came into use with creation and never have, and never can, case their action as long as the Universe exists.

Each of us brings our own radio set with us when we arrive at the station called "Life;" and we are receiving messages constantly whether we recognize the fact or not.

To quote from *Elements of Radio Telephony,* by William C. Ballard, Jr., M. E., (Assistant Professor of Electrical Engineering, Cornell University):

"RADIO RECEIVING EQUIPMENT"

"Tuning—If one will depress the loud pedal on a piano and using some tone of constant pitch while the pedal is down, the set of strings corresponding to that pitch will be set into vibration. This fact can be verified by suddenly stopping the tone and listening intently while the pedal is still held down when the string vibration can be recognized by a faint ringing tone produced by the vibrating strings. The phenomenon, which is known as 'sympathetic vibration,' is the basis of all radio tuning. The transmitter sets up a note in the ether corresponding to the sound produced and this radio 'note' travels out in all directions and impinges on hundreds of antenna systems which correspond to the strings on the piano, but the only ones on which it has any appreciable effect are those which are tuned to the same frequency or wave-length as the transmitted wave."

Exactly as it is with the mechanical radio, so it is with our own physical human *tuner;* the vibratory waves which have the strongest effect upon us are those which are tuned to the *same* frequency and wave lengths as our own.

To *what* we are tuned is an easy matter to discover if we once realized what is happening in Nature.

We *cannot* be born at any time of the year without being tuned to the particular season at which we arrived; and the action going on in Nature at the period of birth allotted to us, will also be going on and continue to go on, at all times and places, in our own human body and the special physical organs governed by those particular radio waves.

There are other points beside that of birth which must be taken into consideration in a close diagnosis of our *tuners;* as we *may* be tuned and usually are, to more than one season or even to all four, but in this work we consider only the one point—*birth.*

SPRING

To take things in order, we begin with Spring and will discover what she is broadcasting to the Universe and her own sympathetic *tuners* in particular.

Those of us who love the woods and have had the pleasure of breakfasting at Spring's table, have long ago learned that the predominating flavor which will be served there will be sour.

The first message, however, sent out by Spring even before the setting of her breakfast table, is her broadcast to vegetation that the morning of the year has dawned and it is time to get up and dress.

Then by slow degrees vegetation opens its sleepy eyes and begins to yawn and stretch and twist itself and otherwise start up its circulation and get its liver into action, in preparation for the business of the day—growing.

Now you whose physical body is tuned to Spring, have a body which is engaged in precisely this action of the renewal of life; rousing, or trying to arouse, liver and circulation and otherwise forcing a continual effort at *starting new growths*.

When, with the Spring awakening, the sap of the tree and plants begins to run, it will produce in that tree or plant a normal condition and growth unless there is some other condition present which is working *against* normality and is stronger in its action than the normal one.

Naturally when this occurs, when there is some obstacle in the way which is hindering a free flow, or some very wrong condition of weather or soil, or any other obstruction, abnormality ensues; and the usual result in the tree is a twisted limb, an ugly knotted formation or some abnormal condition which will forever after be an obstruction to mar the perfect development originally intended. When this takes place in the human body warts, tumors, cancers result.

Harmonious and correct vibration produces harmonious and correct development, mentally and physically; discordant vibrations will tend to produce mental and physical deformities, the extent of these being according to the amount of discord.

This does *not* mean, however, that those born in Spring *must* inevitably, at some period of life, suffer from a disorder of this sort; merely that the tendency is always strongly present and must be guarded against.

Neither does it mean that those having Summer, Autumn or Winter bodies instead of Spring, are absolutely immune in this direction because there are other points beside that of birth which must be taken into consideration in a close diagnosis, but here, as already stated, we are working entirely on the one point.

The message of Spring, therefore, is to awaken Nature from its winter sleep; to start into action the elements and conditions which will produce the growth of vegetation and under the heading "Wood" we will hereafter classify vegetation of every kind, meaning also "Air," as it includes *all* which grows up into the air.

The next step in Spring's message is in regard to color and we cannot for one moment, think of vegetation of the Earth without instantly realizing that the color is *green;* and we are all aware that the emanations from the liver are a greenish yellow, the liver being the principal organ dominated by this season.

Spring's message regarding color, therefore, is extremely plain to all eyes and there can be no dispute concerning it.

To summarize the message when Spring is working at the broadcasting station:

Element predominating—Wood (vegetation)

Action—Growth

Principal flavor—Sour

Organ of the human body most strongly aroused and acted upon—Liver

Color—Green

In both nature and the human body the possibility of Abnormal Growths.

SUMMER

No force in Nature can exist without *producing* some other force outside itself; just as we ourselves cannot exist without having an influence of some kind on our associates and surroundings.

The force, or in other words, element, *produced* by Wood is Fire, and the season following that of Spring has this Element as its particular feature.

None of us can help realizing that Summer represents Heat and therefore *must* be the action of Fire.

Further, if we pause for a moment to think, we will also realize that during this season—or in hot countries—we cannot run and jump and exercise in any violent manner without causing our hearts to overdo their action and our blood to become overheated and circulate too rapidly for our own good.

Those born during the Summer period will carry with them always a tendency to an easily excited heart, overheated blood and too rapid circulation, on the smallest provocation. They should never become athletes or do too much violent exercise even in winter.

Those of us who have had the privilege of investigating and sampling the luncheon dishes provided by Summer, have discovered that much of the vegetation which was sour in Spring has now assumed a bitter flavor and has become strong and more or less fibrous and tough.

In the human body this is the period of developed life when the soft bending tissues of the child have turned into the stronger ones of the adult.

In this case again there is no possibility of our going wrong on color; for if there is one point of which we are all perfectly sure, it is that the color of Fire is red, speaking generally.

The action of Fire of course, is to make things hot, and the blood of the person born in summer will be more easily overheated than that of those born at other periods, while the further tendency is to dryness.

The author has seen this so strongly shown that the body never perspired no matter how hot the weather.

The natural further result is that those having a Summer body will be thrown into fevers with very little trouble and on what in another person, would be small provocation.

Summer's radio message is, therefore, in brief:

Element—Fire

Action—Heat

Principal flavor—Bitter

Organ of the body most strongly aroused and acted upon—Heart

Color—Red

EARTH, THE CENTER

When a fire is burning—and the stronger the fire the truer this is—it is producing ashes; or in other words, Earth.

That Earth could not exist without its central fires we are fully aware, and that this planet would cease to be habitable if these fires were ever to go out.

So, as Wood produces Fire, Fire produces Earth.

Earth represents the *center* upon which we live, from which and through which all our means of sustenance are derived and over, or around which, the seasons pass each year.

Most of us know that an electrical current must be "grounded," that is, connected with and into the earth. Just as it is in the universal action about us, so—as we are also a part of the same universal action—it is with our human body. We must "ground" our life currents through our own individual center; that physical organ in our bodies which represents the element Earth.

Now where *do* we "ground" the materials necessary to keep our central fire in action and our life currents in working order?

Through our stomach, of course; and as Fire produces Earth, so does the fuel we put in our furnace produce the strength of our physical body; or, to put it in another form, the *personal* earth which we inhabit and which belongs to us alone.

There are certain periods when the Earth is especially active; when it is producing at its fullest, or preparing itself for the coming year, or resting or performing some other action necessary to the various forms of functioning it must be ready for throughout the year.

These periods occur the *last* month of each season—the *last* month of the three months of Spring, the *last* month of Summer, the last month of Autumn, the *last* month of Winter.

Should the birth be, for instance, the last month of Spring, the organs dominating our liver *and* stomach.

Should it be the last month of Summer, it will indicate heart *and* stomach.

This will be equally true of the two seasons remaining, Autumn and Winter, which we have not mentioned.

The particular function of Earth is to harmonize and sweeten, in other words, to reduce the elements necessary to our existence to a state where they can harmonize and work together in the manner best suited to the sustaining of physical life.

It represents, principally, the starches, and in flavors, sweet. In color, yellow.

Station Earth is therefore broadcasting:

Element—Earth

Action—Harmonizing

Principal flavor—Sweet

Organ of the body most strongly aroused and acted upon—Stomach

Color—Yellow

AUTUMN

As each element must in the natural course of events produce another, so Earth is producing *Metal*.

When Summer has finished her work of providing the heat necessary for growth and ripening and in general making ready for the harvest, she begins to let her fires cool down and prepare for her winter's rest, while Autumn steps in to attend to the next few months of work.

The result of a fire dying out in a stove or furnace is of course the cooling of, and finally *cold* metal; this is exactly the condition brought in by Autumn—cooling, and later on, cold metal.

So Autumn means really, cold radiations from chilling metal, and these produce a harsh effect on the lungs, and it is an actual fact that those born at this time of year will be more readily subject to tubercular and other lung troubles than their Spring or Summer brothers.

The color assigned to this season by the ancient teaching is *white,* as at this period the year is forming the white conditions which later lead to the snow of the coming winter. In other words the year is *turning white.*

WHITE

We are familiar with the universal title of tuberculosis—the "Great *White* Plague" but we are not all aware, according to statements made to the author by many physicians in high standing, that this is precisely the condition present in tuberculosis; the blood corpuscles are turning *white.*

The cold metal radiations produce exactly the *flavor* which results when we hold a piece of metal in our mouth long enough to acquire the *acrid* taste known as metallic.

Autumn then is broadcasting to the world for those who have ears to hear, or rather a mind open enough to receive its message:

Element—Metal (meaning radiations resulting from chilled metal)

Action—Cooling off, or chilling

Organ of the human body most strongly aroused and acted upon—Lungs

Principal flavor—Acrid

Color—White

Danger of easily-taken colds which tend to settle on the lungs.

WINTER

Metal, by volatilization taking place internally in the depths of the earth, produces liquid, or to place it under the heading we prefer to use —Water; resulting in the snow and ice, rain and cold, and other clammy and watery conditions of the next season, Winter. Therefore, as before, one element is producing another which in this case is Water.

During this season the tendency is to slowness, congealing, stopping; the year is entering its resting period, growing drowsy, entering into its winter's sleep; and as this condition is occurring in Nature, so it is occurring in the physical body of the person who has entered life at this period; the whole action will be slower than that of the former seasons and the physical conditions turn to a *slow* heart action, just as those of the Summer give the tendency to over-rapid action. The other organs to which this season directs its attention are the kidneys.

As in the former cases if the birth occurs in the third or last month of Winter, the message will then read, stomach and kidneys; while if it be the third or last month of *Autumn* it will read, stomach and lungs.

The *color* of Winter shows itself plainly to those who are on the lookout for what Winter has to say, through the dark days, gloom and generally prevailing *blackness*. It is, in other words, the *shadow* resulting from the sunlight and quite as necessary to life as the sun itself.

As the Spring and Summer represent the fullness of the year's day, so does Autumn give the late afternoon and Winter the night, darkness, blackness, the period of rest and sleep.

The *flavor* which accompanies Winter is again found by searching where it will be most distinctly shown, in the great *Waters* of the earth, the seas and oceans, and the answer is of course *salt;* just as we all know that *tears* are salt and the expresion "weeping salt tears" is in common use.

The message of Winter therefore is:
Element—Water
Action—Soaking and descending
Principal flavor—Salt
Organ of the body most strongly aroused and acted upon—Kidneys
Color—Black or dark brown
Possibility of kidney troubles or too slow action of the heart.

If we place a seed in the ground the first necessary action is to Water it in order to start the *growth,* and as in the case of the other elements it has been shown that each one *must* produce another, so *Water* produces Wood or Vegetation, as we already know the results to vegetation in years of lack of rain.

We will now take these elements from another side.

Just as each element produces another so does each *conquer* another.

To begin, as before, with Spring: Wood, the element of this season, must have a source from which to grow. To obtain this it utilizes Earth and makes it its servant or helper, as one wishes to call it; it *conquers* Earth and uses it for its own purposes in order to supply the demands of the other forms of life which are dependent upon it. When in its normal condition, where it can spread in its best and most natural manner, it *covers* the Earth.

Therefore the radio message further reads:

The element Wood *conquers* the element Earth.

Summer gives us the element Fire and in order to be of any use to humanity Metal must be put through Fire; it must be melted in Fire in order to be constructed into useful or beautiful objects. Metal therefore, is *conquered* by Fire.

The element Fire conquers the element Metal.

Earth overcomes or conquers Water by the process of absorption, so:

The element Earth conquers the element Water.

Water requires almost no discussion on this point as we all know without telling that:

The element Water conquers the element Fire. (The first desire of a fever patient is for water.)

We have now but one element left, that of Wood; Wood to be utilized must be *cut into pieces* by the use of Metal; the harvest must be reaped by the use of Metal; so:

The element of Metal conquers that of Wood.

Each of these elements carry with them certain other qualities which we will at once recognize as they are mentioned, as we see them in action about us all through life, in every direction, only our attention may never have been called to the matter.

The action of Wood is *bend* and *straighten,* even as the branches and grasses bend and straighten in the wind or in the process of growing.

Its quality is to *nourish.*

Fire or heat, as again we all know, rises; just as in fever one of the first indications is a very red *face* and hot *head;* its action is to *blaze* and *ascend.*

Its quality is to *penetrate.*

The action connected with Earth is that of sowing and reaping, or to bring about the harmonizing action necessary to keep life going.

The action of Metal is to yield and resist; to be one moment soft and another hard. Its quality is to destroy. In other words to bring about the destruction of the food we use to sustain life, in such a manner as to render it perfect for our use.

The action of Water is to soak and descend; water as we know *always* runs down, never up; and in kidney troubles the indications begin in the feet and legs, the exact reverse of those of fever.

Its quality is to *strengthen.*

To further complete the full message of the wonderful seasons as they come and go each year, we divide the points of the compass in the usual manner, east, south, west and north, and follow out the same idea in the body itself by right half, upper half, left half and lower half.

To the east belongs the Spring and the right half of the body; to the south the Summer and the upper half of the body; to the west the Autumn and the left half of the body; to the north the Winter and the lower half of the body.

The proper arrangement of all life, physical or mental, is *even balance,* or as close to an even balance as we can attain; in other words correct proportions. We should have the right amount of water to keep our bodies in health. Too much or too little means physical ills. We require the proper amount of food (vegetation, *wood*) and the right sort, or the result again is physical ills. We must get from our food the necessary amount of *metal* (chemicals in various forms) or our body suffers.

In the same manner as our "outward and physical body" suffers from any wrong proportion of the many constituents which enter into its combination and maintenance, so also does our "inward and spiritual body" suffer in like degree from the same wrong conditions. In other words, we may have too much or too little *water;* too much or too little *wood;* too much or too little *fire;* too much or too little *earth.*

This will bring about wrong mental and physical conditions in the *circumstances* of the life.

To quote from the Shu-king: "No configuration is perfect unless the five elements work in it harmoniously: Water, fire, wood, metal, earth.

Whenever fire or heat predominate, disaster will ensue unless it is counterbalanced by another element such as water. If the element earth is overruled by water, or suffers from want of water, there is no fecundation, no production of food and raiment; crops are devasted. In this case the entire element *wood* may be destroyed. Fire and water, when united in harmony and in adequate proportions, further fecundation."

In the beginning Spring was referred to as the early morning, the hours from midnight to sunrise, the dawning of another year. The year, as it has so often been called, *is* but a *long* day.

The four periods of a day are, midnight to sunrise (*spring*); sunrise to noon (*summer,* its beginning and height); noon to sunset (early and late *autumn*); the *day* falling asleep—*dying* —in the West (Free-Masons will understand this); sunset to midnight, the resting time of the day (*winter,* death), the resting time of the year, when all *life* is preparing for another *day,* or another year.

As the day, so is the year; as the year so is human life. The hours from midnight to sunrise, from sunrise to noon, then slowly falling asleep in the West, to waken with the rising of the Resurrection Sun, into—the new day, the new year, the new life.

The truth is always simple. Those who see and understand the true science of the rising and the setting sun seek no further. They have *found*.

CHAPTER VII

The Connection of Names with Music and the Action of Notes and Chords Upon Your Life

WOULDST thou know if a people be well governed, if its laws be good or bad? Examine the music it practises."
—*Confucius*.

"Airs of an age of disorder indicate dissatisfaction and anger.

"Of good order, composure and enjoyment. Of a state going to ruin, sorrow and troubled thought. There is an interaction between the words and airs of a people and the character of their government.

"If the five notes are all irregular and injuriously interfere with one another, they indicate a state of insolent disorder and at no distant date extinction and ruin.

"Beasts know sound but not its modulations; the masses of common people know modulations but not music.

"Similarity and union are the aim of music; difference and distinction that of ceremony. From union comes mutual affection. From difference mutual respect.

"Where music prevails we find a weak coa-

lescence; where ceremony, a tendency to separate. It is the business of the two to blend.

"Music comes from within and ceremonies
from without. Music produces stillness of mind.
Ceremonies the elegancies of manner.

"The highest style of music is distinguished
by its ease. The highest form of elegance by
its undemonstrativeness.

"Notes that die away quickly characterize
small aims, the people's thoughts are sad.

"When generosity, harmony, and placid easy
temper prevail, the notes are varied and elegant,
with frequent changes; people are satisfied and
pleased.

"When coarse, violent, excitable, the notes
vehement at first and distinct in the end, and
are full and bold throughout the piece, people
are resolute and daring.

"When pure and straightforward, strong
and correct, the notes are grave, and expressive
of sincerity; people are self-controlled and re-
spectful.

"When magnanimity, placidity and kindness
prevail, the notes are natural, full, harmonious;
the people affectionate and loving.

"When the ruler is careless, disorderly, perverse and dissipated, the notes are tedious and
ill-regulated and the people proceed to excesses
and disorder.

"Whenever evil and depraved notes affect
men, a corresponding evil spirit responds to
them, and when this evil spirit accomplishes its

manifestations, licentious music is the result."

"Whenever correct notes affect men, a correct spirit responds and harmonious music is the result.

"The initiating cause and the result correspond to each other.

"The round and the deflected, the crooked and the straight, have each its own category and affect one another according to their class.

"Fine, distinct notes image Heaven. Ample and grand, earth. When the superior man uses and exhibits his ceremonies and music, Heaven and earth will respond by displaying their brilliant energies.

"When the wind is moved to sorrow the sound is sharp and fading away. Pleasure slow and gentle. Joy exclamatory and soon disappears. Anger, coarse and fierce. Reverence, straightforward with indications of humility. Love, harmonious and soft."*

Every sound is a note of music; each note of music has its responsive notes, as all musicians and scientists know.

To repeat from the French of Rodolphe Radau "Sound is movement. Repose is dumb. All sound, all noise, tells of motion; it is the invisible telegraph which nature uses."

With apologies to Radau, we take the liberty of *transposing* his phrase. *Movement* is *sound.* Any *motion,* however slight, tells of *sound.* The

---

*See the Li Ki. Sacred books of the East. Max Muller.

sound may be too delicate to reach *our* ear, but it is none the less present, making itself felt on the surrounding atmosphere, striking its own note, and calling into action its own responsive or sympathetic notes. Therefore, to quote from the preceding chapter, each portion of the body, however minute, each action, "condition, feeling or emotion, however slight, is under the influence of a note, or chord, of music. Its own keynote or scale."

The late Dr. Henry C. Houghton, whose work as a specialist made him one of the lights of his school, based his method of treatment almost entirely upon this fact of a personal keynote of vibration. He was a member of that famous class which produced William Todd Helmuth and other stars of first magnitude in the medical world.

As the body, so is the earth; each atmospheric condition has its own keynote, therefore, of course, each season.

Winter and darkness—night of the year and of the day—is the tone *d*.

Spring—the time before the dawn of the year—is the tone *a;* as is the same period of the day.

Summer and noon—the full height of the year and of the day—is the tone *c*.

Autumn—the ripened crops, the harvest, the time of the coming home to rest, before the deeper refreshing sleep of the night—is the tone *g*.

Above, under, through all these tones, is that of the earth, sounding its own creating tone of *f*.*

"Says Silliman, in his *Principle of Physics:* 'The aggregate sound of Nature, as heard in the roar of a distant city, or the waving of a large forest, is said to be a single definite tone of appreciable pitch. This tone is held to be the middle *f* of the pianoforte, which may therefore be considered the keynote of Nature.'"

As we ourselves are *tuned,* so do the various seasons, atmospheric conditions, friends, companies, climate, environments, affect us "for better, for worse."

As each season has its individual tone, it will be even more readily seen that it must have pitch; summer, of course, the highest; winter the lowest. In the same manner does each portion of our bodies respond also to its pitch. As we all know, there are "highly strung" people, and those strung on a low pitch; those who keep us at a high tension; those who "unstring" every nerve and bring us to the lowest point of depression.

Abnormality is produced by being out of tune. If we are in tune *ourselves,* we cannot be out of tune with the Universe, because in *it* is encompassed all tones, *all* chords, *all* keys. *Our* lives will play a melody whether others do

---

*At the end of the definitions (for the advanced use of these numbers in connection with the zodiacal houses and the different periods of birth) "The Chartoscope" will prove invaluable.

BIBLIOGRAPHY

SOUND

Works of Robert Boyle
Sound and Music..SEDLEY TAYLOR
Sensations of Tone..H. L. F. HELMHOLTZ
Students' Musical Acoustics.........................H. L. F. HELMHOLTZ
How the Voice Looks.......................................PROF. SCRIPTURE
Science in Nature...ZAHM
Visible Sound ....CENTURY MAGAZINE
Quabbalah ....ISSAC MYER
Wonders of Science.......................................RODOLPHE RADAN
Hidden Way Across the Threshold.........................J. C. STREET

MUSIC

Chinese Music ....AMOIT
Chinese Music ....VAN AALST
The Li Ki..CHINESE CLASSICS
What is Music........PROF. ISSAC RICE (COLUMBIA UNIVERSITY)
Science in Nature...ZAHM
Sensations of Tone..HELMHOLTZ
Student's Musical Acoustics.......................................HOLMHOLTZ
Sound and Music...SEDLEY TAYLOR
Principles of Physics..SILLIMAN
What is Music?..PROF. ISAAC L. RICE

EGYPTIAN

History of Egypt...H. K. BRUGSCH
La Livre de ce qu 'il y a dans l' Hades........GUSTAVE JEQUIER
Researches on the Great Pyramid......................W. M. F. PETRIE
Pyramidographia ....JOHN GREAVES
History of Egypt ....JAMES H. BREASTED
Egyptian Inscriptions ....A. E. WEIGELLS
Book of the Master of The Secret House, W. MARSHAM ADAMS
Egypt ....MARTIN BRIMMER
Oldest Book in the World..ISAAC MYER
La Divinities Egyptienne...............................OLIVIER BEAUREGARD
Book of The Dead...E. A. W. BUDGE
The Egyptian Heaven and Hell.........................E. A. W. BUDGE

COLOR

Principles of Light and Color........................E. D. Babbitt, M.D.
Chromatic Aesthetics ....George Field
Symbolic Color ....Baron F. de Portal
Physics ....Sir David Brewster
Elementary Color ....Milton Bradley
Color Harmony and Contrast.....................................James Ward

LIGHT

Optics ....Sir David Brewster
Researches on Light...Robert Hunt
Physics ....Silliman

CHINESE

Religious Systems of China.............................J. J. M. de Groot
Chinese Readers' Manual ....W. F. Mayers
Le Yi-King; or, Livre des Changements de la Dynastie
    des Tschon Par ....P. L. F. Philastre
Yi-King ....J. B. Regis
Le Yik-King ....C. J. de Harlez, D.D.
Textes Taoistes, Par..................................Chas. de Harlez, D.D.
The Tao Teh King
Texts of Taoism...James Legge
Choo-He 1130-1200
Confucian Cosmogöny ....Rev. Thos. McClatchie
The Yi-King of the Chinese.....................................J. Edkins
The Yi-King (Sacred Book of the East)................James Legge
Taoist Texts ....Frederic H. Balfour
Religion in China ....J. M. de Groot
Lao Tsze ....John Chalmers
The Thai-Shang ....James Legge
Texts of Taoism...James Legge
Le Texte Originaire du Yih-King.....................C. F. Harlez
Les Figures Symbolique du Yi-King......................C. F. Harley
The Oldest Book of the
    Chinese ....Baron Albert Terrien de Lacouperie
The Shu-King

HEBREW

Kabbalah Unveiled ....MacGregor Mathers
La Clef du Zohar...Albert Jonnet
Quabbalah ....Isaac Myers
La Clef des Grande Mysteres..................................Eliphas Levi
Le Livre des Splendeurs..................................Eliphas Levi
Le Cabbale ....M. Gerard Encausse (Papus)
Tarot of the Bohemians..................................Gerard Encausse
Macounerie Occulte ....Ragan
                    and many others

CPSIA information can be obtained
at www.ICGtesting.com
Printed in the USA
BVOW09s0958171117

500684BV00016B/888/P